THE IMPACT OF ORGANIZATIONAL CAPITAL INVESTMENT ON EMPLOYEE INNOVATION IN THE MANUFACTURING INDUSTRY

Dr. Hyacinth Nwachukwu

authorHOUSE®

AuthorHouse™
1663 Liberty Drive
Bloomington, IN 47403
www.authorhouse.com
Phone: 1 (800) 839-8640

Published by AuthorHouse 05/10/2016

ISBN: 978-1-5246-0703-6 (sc)
ISBN: 978-1-5246-0702-9 (e)

Library of Congress Control Number: 2016907284

Print information available on the last page.

Any people depicted in stock imagery provided by Thinkstock are models, and such images are being used for illustrative purposes only. Certain stock imagery © Thinkstock.

This book is printed on acid-free paper.

THE IMPACT OF ORGANIZATIONAL CAPITAL INVESTMENT
ON EMPLOYEE INNOVATION IN THE MANUFACTURING
INDUSTRY

Abstract of Doctoral Dissertation Research

Submitted to the
Faculty of Argosy University, Phoenix Campus

In Partial Fulfillment of
the Requirements for the Degree of

Doctor of Business Administration

by

Hyacinth Umunnakwe Nwachukwu

Argosy University

December 2015

Matthew Kuofie, MBA, PhD

Richard Dool, PhD

Dale J. Mancini, PhD

Department: College of Business

Abstract

This study involved an exploration of the impact of organizational capital investment on employee innovation in the manufacturing industry. The overarching question was: Does organizational capital investment impact employee innovation in the manufacturing industry? Organizations tend to place much emphasis on how skill drives innovation, but not on how capital investment impact employee innovation. The research was guided using a qualitative phenomenological case study design to probe the impact of capital investment on employee innovation. Participants were selected through a convenience and purposive sampling method using the researcher's personal professional network as well as the snowball method to seek participants from individuals' referrals. Data collection involved personal interviews, audio recording, and note taking. The assumption was that employee innovation is not an option but a necessity, because organizations compete on global fronts for resources and market share. Consequently, capital investment in machinery and employee innovation becomes symbiotic in nature, not mutually exclusive. Results showed employee innovation can be impacted and enhanced through the acquisition and application of appropriate technological capital investment. The researcher recommends further research to ascertain whether the amount of organizational capital investment is proportional to the development of employee innovativeness.

Acknowledgements

The writing of this dissertation is the culmination of the researcher's efforts that have been accumulating over a significant period of time. The end result of a doctoral program is the dissertation itself.

The responsibility of the research rests solely with the researcher. However, the product of this painstaking assignment must invariably be credited to some worthy individuals. It is important to mention here that I was extremely fortunate to have the competent and sympathetic assistance of my dissertation chairman and co-chairman in the persons of Dr. Matthews Kuofie and Dr. Richard Doo, respectively, who have diligently and didactically worked with me throughout the exhaustive period of this scholarly journey. For this reason, I say thanks to all of you!

I would also like to thank Dr. Dale Mancini, who served as my mentor and was instrumental in the selection of my dissertation topic; Dr. Peter Egwom, who served as my counsel in time of need; my editor, Amy Gralewski; and my financial and academic advisors, Anthony Memole and Jennifer Lee-Hooper, respectively, for their guidance.

My final thanks should go to my lovely wife, Lolo Regina N. Nwachukwu, who stood behind me all these years and provided both financial and moral support, but sometimes drove me crazy with her evangelical rhetoric; last, but not the least, my baby son, Victor Chizuru Nwachukwu, who served as my IT consultant, and my beloved daughter, Dr. Judith Eze-nwanyi Nwachukwu Anadu for her support. I sincerely remain grateful for their valuable contributions in making this dissertation task a success.

Dedication

This book is dedicated to all my children: Ezenwanyi, Ikechukwu, Kelechi, Chimaroke, Uchenna and Chizuru (Enyinnaya), and to my grand-children, Kobichukwu (Uzodimma), and Kambi (Ada-nna-nna); lastly to my dear friends, Dr. Peter Onu and Sir Martins Nwamadi. These people helped in one way or the other in making my world more meaningful.

Table of Contents

Abstract...vii

Acknowledgements..ix

Dedication xi

Chapter One: Introduction 1

Problem Statement 2

Purpose of the Study 3

Research Questions...3

Limitations of the Study...4

Delimitations of the Study 4

Definitions of Terms 4

Capital Investment 4

Innovation...5

Intellectual Capital 5

Research and Development (R&D) 5

Return on Investment (ROI) 5

Structural Capital..5

Significance of the Study..5

Chapter Two: Review of the Literature...7

Background of the Problem...8

Theoretical Foundation..12

Theories and Models Relating to Capital Investment and
Innovation...15

Theory of Capital Investment...15

Theory of Human Innovation 15

Review of the Literature 17

Summary 19

Chapter Three: Methodology 21

Research Questions...21

Research Methodology..22

Research Design...22

Population and Sample Selection 23

Instrumentation...23

Demographic questions (DQs) 23

Interview questions (IQs) 24

Follow-up questions (FQs)..25

Quality Criteria 25
Reliability and Validity...............................26
Data Collection Procedures 27
Procedure 30
Data Analysis Procedures 30
Ethical Considerations 31
Informed Consent 31
Confidentiality and Anonymity.................32
Limitations of the Study...................................32
Delimitations of the Study 32
Summary 33
Potential Benefits of the Study.........................33
Participants...33
Professional Community 34
Chapter Four: Results 35
Restatement of the Purpose 35
Restatement of the Problem...............................35
Summary of the Study Methodology.................36
Study Design 36
Instrumentation..36
Participants...36
Participant Demographics 36
Research Sub Question 1 38
Interview question 1 38
Interview question 4...................................40
Interview question 5...................................40
Research Sub Question 2 43
Research Sub Question 3 44
Summary 45
Success and Growth of the Economy..........45
Enhanced Employee Retention 45
Job Satisfaction...46
Cost Reduction and Quality Improvement..............46
Enhanced Knowledge and Skills.................46
Absence of Bureaucratic Bottleneck and Overhead ... 46
Chapter Five: Summary, Conclusions, and Recommendations......47
Background of the Problem................................47
Summary of Findings...52

    Conclusions...54
    Recommendation for Further Studies...................55

References 57
Appendices...63
A. Interview Questions..63
B. Consent Form...65

Table of Tables

1. RSQs vs. Interview Questions 28
2. RSQs vs. Data Analysis 31
3. Demographics of Participants...37
4. Respondents' Answers to Interview Question 1 39
5. Respondents' Answers to Interview Questions 4 and 5 41
6. Respondents' Answers to Interview Questions 6 and 7 42

Chapter One

Introduction

The first chapter of any dissertation is considered the most critical as it is intended to give a clear view of the context of the study, and other related factors that follow depend largely on how well this particular chapter is designed and structured (Creswell, 2007). Chapter 1 contains details of the problem background, purpose, and research questions, thus setting the stage for unveiling the overall problem under investigation (Booth, Colomb, & Williams, 2005; Creswell, 2007).

Technology and industrialization can be said to have given rise to the globalization of trade, consequently making it possible for the international economic community to initiate and embrace capital investment strategies cum trade negotiation as championed by the World Trade Organization (WTO) and other international and regional trading blocs (Manyika & Pelissie du Rausas, 2011). The idea is to remove trade barriers among trading partners and stimulate global economic growth. This stimulation of a global economy, in a chain reaction, triggered the desire of leaders of multinational corporations (MNCs) to reconsider their organizational capital investment strategies in relation to employee innovation (Marimuthu, Arokiasamy, & Ismail, 2009). For example, the creation of the Internet, a situation attributable to employee innovation, accounted for significant growth in global productivity, thus adding about 3.4% to global gross domestic product (GDP; Manyika & Pelissie du Rausas, 2011). Therefore, the discussion of the impacts of organizational capital investment on employee innovation will not be complete without reference to the technology and enterprise competitiveness that drive employee innovation (Marimuthu et al., 2009; Rastogi, 2002).

Innovation can emanate from creative ideas, and creative ideas can be enhanced by the application of technology in the form of organizational capital investment. The capacity of a firm to innovate, both in human resource and organizational capital investment (i.e., plant, machinery, and equipment), can be seen as a fundamental process toward the attainment of competitive advantage and economies of scale over other competitors within the same industry (Tether, Mina, Consoli, & Gagliardi, 2005).

Employee innovation can be considered a natural phenomenon, though it can be complemented through the application of exogenous auxiliary resources such as technology, machinery, and equipment, thereby leading to organizational, human, and technological innovation (Pyka & Esben, 2013). This form of organizational philosophy tends to provide an enabling environment for firms to develop and exploit opportunities for employee innovation and eradicate inertia emanating from radical shifts in capital investment strategies and unfavorable technological changes. In the actual sense of the word, the term employee innovation portends creative resource and idea generation that leads to the transformation of values relative to the production of goods and services (Davila, Epstein, & Shelton, 2006). It places more emphasis on initiating new ideas and putting them into gainful use (Mexias & Glynn, 1993).

Problem Statement

A good number of researchers have addressed the issue of organizational capital investment relative to job performance (Davila et al., 2006; Nelson & Pack, 1999). However, these researchers failed to provide a critical assessment of the impact of organizational capital investment on employee innovation. After a comprehensive review of existing literature related to the current study topic of the impact of organizational capital investment on employee innovation in the manufacturing industry, it became apparent that this topic was worthy of investigation. However, it is important to point out specifically that the gap in the literature as reviewed relates to the fact that research has not been conducted regarding the impact of capital investment on employee innovation in the manufacturing industry. This particular study was designed explore this as a new theory to contribute to the field of business administration. Therefore, the problem statement points to the fact that it is not known how organizational capital investment impacts employee innovation in the manufacturing industry. Additionally, this research was designed to shed more light on how organizations identify and create the appropriate capital investment, and promote an enabling environment that is conducive for employee innovation (Davila et al., 2006).

Purpose of the Study

The purpose of the current study was to address the unanswered questions confronting leaders of competing firms in the industry. That is, whether organizational capital investment impacts employee innovation, as it is not known how capital investment impacts employee innovation in the manufacturing industry. Also, it is important to note that most organizations place much emphasis on how skills drive innovation but give little or no attention to how organizational capital investment impacts employee innovation. The research design employed was a qualitative study utilizing semi-structured interviews with 16 professionals who met the following criteria: male or female engineers, marketing managers, accounting managers, financial managers, and production/operational managers who were 25 years or older, with at least 5 years of on the job experience and a minimum of a high school diploma. Participants were drawn mostly from a population of 65 members of various manufacturing plants in Baltimore, Maryland.

The participants were interviewed, using a list of interview questions, and the resulting data were extracted and analyzed to provide answers to each of the research sub questions listed in the next section. This enabled the researcher to gain a clear understanding of whether or not organizational capital investment impacts employee innovation in the manufacturing industry. Therefore, the purpose of the investigation was to fill the gap in the literature and ascertain the impacts of organizational capital investment on employee innovation in the manufacturing industry.

Research Questions

The overall research question used to guide this study was: Does organizational capital investment impact employee innovation in the manufacturing industry? It should, however, be noted that the data collected from the research sub questions (RSQs) were analyzed to address and provide answer to the overall research question (Booth et al., 2005; Creswell, 2007; Richards & Morse, 2007). This concept is called triangulation (Creswell, 2007).

The RSQs considered in the study were as follows:

RSQ1: What are the most important factors that are favorable for employee innovation?

RSQ2: What are the most critical elements of organizational capital investment?

RSQ3: Are there any managing challenges regarding capital investment and employee innovation?

Limitations of the Study

The study had certain limitations that were out of the researcher's control. They were as follows:

- There was a time constraint in which the researcher needed to complete the dissertation research.
- There was a financial constraint in completing the dissertation research.
- The researcher had no control over the responses the participants provided to the interview questions.
- The study was limited to one firm, making it hard to generalize the results.

Delimitations of the Study

Delimitations refer to conditions over which the researcher has control and uses to set the boundaries of the study. They were as follows:

- A sample of 16 professional engineers and managers from Baltimore, Maryland, was used.
- The participants came from the researcher's personal professional network and had a minimum of 5 years of on the job experience.
- This was a qualitative study.
- Participants had a minimum of a high school education.

Definitions of Terms

Below are definitions of the terms used in this research study.

Capital Investment

Funds invested in a company for the purpose of promoting the short- and long-term objectives of the business. It can refer to a company's acquisition of capital assets, such as fixed assets, and employee training.

Capital investment was divided into two categories for the purpose of this study––intangible intellectual capital (e.g., employee innovation/

human capital) and tangible structural capital investment (e.g., machinery and equipment).

Innovation

Innovation can be defined as a conceptual framework for converting research into a physical product for commercialization (Davila et al., 2006). In buttressing this definition, Davila et al. (2006) noted, "nor is it solely about processes and stage-gate tools." These do count, but tools and processes alone are not effective . . . they must be coupled with an organization, metrics, and rewards that can make things happen" (p. xviii).

Intellectual Capital

Stewart (2010) defined intellectual capital as "collective brainpower," which includes intangible resources such as patent of ideas.

Research and Development (R&D)

Can be considered to be an investigative activity that a business or firm adopts with the intention to discover and develop a new line of products or services.

Return on Investment (ROI)

A performance indicator or measure employed to evaluate the investment efficiency of a certain number of investment portfolios.

Structural Capital

This Includes tangible assets, such as organizational infrastructure, processes, and assets (Ross, 1998). In terms of measurable factors, the resources expended in research and developments (R&D) were used as important factors for capital investment whereas the value of the physical products arising from R&D was considered as the output key factor for value measurement of innovation. Also, other tangible capital investments, such as land, labor, entrepreneur, and capital, should be taken into account and considered as auxiliaries to employee innovation.

Significance of the Study

The significance of this qualitative study is to help organizational leaders to determine whether organizational capital investment impacts employee innovation in the manufacturing industry.

The results are intended to address the gap in the literature of the impact of organizational capital investment on employee innovation in the manufacturing industry. If organizational capital investment enhances employee innovation, then results from this study will enable organizations to increase organizational capital investment to enhance employee innovation. Results also address the capital investment factors that enhance employee innovation.

Another implication of the study is that results will be beneficial to the success and growth of industries and the economy. This is true because when employee innovation is transformed into valuable tangible goods and services, consumer demands and interest are generated; consequently, jobs are created and the economy benefits.

Another implication is the results can be used to help determine the limit of organizational capital investment on employees' training that enhances their innovation. Employee innovation can improve organizational competitiveness, value, and growth. This can stem from robust investment in R&D; data from 27 U.S. export oriented firms in 2000 to 2007 indicated that these firms attracted highly-skilled jobs during the economic downturn while firms that were non-innovative and had less investment in R&D lost jobs (Ulku, 2004). Sales and productivity per employee in the R&D intensive firms more than doubled that in non-R&D firms. It stands to reason that R&D intensive firms spent more on capital investment as opposed to non-R&D firms (2.2% on capital investment per employee; Ulku, 2004).

The study was also designed to reveal possible managing challenges regarding capital investment and employee innovation. The implication is that if challenges do exist, company leaders should be able to develop strategies to address those management challenges. Future implication of the strategies may lead to new theory to contribute to the field of business administration.

Chapter Two

Review of the Literature

The purpose of this chapter is to present the results of a critical examination of the literature related to the study topic of the impacts of organizational capital investment on employee innovation in the manufacturing industry. The review of the literature was based on previous studies to identify the gap addressed by the current study. This chapter also contains an overview of capital investment and innovation models, as well as a framework that addresses the impact of organizational capital investment on employee innovation.

Technology and industrialization gave rise to the globalization of trade (Davila et al., 2006). Consequently, it became possible for the international community to initiate and embrace trade negotiations. Global trade is being championed by the WTO and other international and regional trading blocs (Manyika & Pelissie du Rausas, 2011). The idea is to remove trade barriers among trading partners and stimulate global economic growth (Davila et al., 2006). This stimulation of a global economy has produced a ripple effect, triggering the desire for leaders of MNCs to reconsider their organizational capital investment portfolios in relation to employee innovation (Manyika & Pelissie du Rausas, 2011). For example, the creation of the Internet accounted for significant growth in global productivity, thus adding about 3.4% to global GDP, a development attributable to employee innovation (Manyika & Pelissie du Rausas, 2011). Therefore, any discussion of the impacts of organizational capital investment on employee innovation will not be complete without reference to the technology and enterprise competitiveness that drive employee innovation (Marimuthu et al., 2009; Rastogi, 2002). Technology involves the transformation process of capital, labor, and entrepreneurship into products and services of desired value (Christensen, 2003). The concept of technology in this context goes beyond engineering to include a range of capital investment and production processes known as innovation (Christensen, 2003).

Innovation can emanate from creativity, and creativity can be enhanced by the application of technology in the form of organizational capital investment (Marimuthu et al., 2009; Rastogi, 2002). The capacity of a firm to innovate, both in human resource and organizational capital investment (i.e., plant, machinery, and equipment), can be seen as a fundamental process toward the attainment of competitive advantage and economies of scale over other competitors within the same industry (Tether et al., 2005).

The term employee innovation portends creative resource or idea generation that leads to the transformation of values relative to the production of goods and services (Davila et al., 2006). However, employee innovation can be considered a natural phenomenon that can be complemented through the application of exogenous auxiliary resources such as technology, machinery, and equipment, thus leading to organizational, human, and technological innovation (Pyka & Esben, 2013). This form of organizational philosophy tends to provide an enabling environment for firms to develop and exploit opportunities for employee innovation, and eradicate inertia emanating from radical shifts in capital investment strategies and unfavorable technological changes (Pyka & Esben, 2013). Employee innovation places more emphasis on initiating new ideas and putting them into gainful use (Mexias & Glynn, 1993).

Background of the Problem

Organizational capital investment is a critical input in strengthening productivity and enhancing employee innovation (Hacklin, Marxt, & Fahrni, 2006). Therefore, the problem in the current study is that it is not known how organizational capital investment impacts employee innovation in the manufacturing industry. Additionally, this research is designed to shed more light on how organizations identify the appropriate capital investment and promote an enabling environment that is conducive for employee innovation (Davila et al., 2006). Keeley (2006) gave a broader theoretical perspective on how innovation links with technology in terms of organizational capital investment. The general characteristics of this link demand that any innovative process tends to provide a meaningful solution to a problem (Keeley, 2006). The linkages are invaluable changes that are in the best interest of the organization relative to time and cost savings (Keeley, 2006).

Early theories on organizational capital investment were concerned with data collection for the measurement and adoption of appropriate business models. For example, Becker (2004) adopted firm level data while Adams, Bessant, and Phelps (2006) adopted the establishment level data system. Becker, in his theory, could not establish that investment in employee education was analogous to employee innovation. In other words, it has not been clearly established that the value of employee innovation is the result of organizational capital investment in machinery and equipment (Adams et al., 2006; Corrado, Hulten, & Sichel, 2004; Tidd, Bessant, & Pavitt, 2005).

A synthesis of the literature also revealed that some researchers disagree with the notion that the availability of capital investment in equipment affords employees the opportunity to interact with innovators in their respective fields (De Angelis & Harvie, 2009; Swanson, 2001; Tidd et al., 2005). Black and Lynch (2004) posited that the main problem with this theory hinges on the adoption of appropriate business strategies relative to organizational structure.

However, recent studies, such as those conducted by Hamel (2012), Thota and Munir (2011), De Angelis and Harvie (2009), Adamson (2009a), and Foucault (2008), point to the fact that organizational capital investment could have a vital impact on employee innovation when appropriately harnessed and managed. This theory lends support to the Schumpeterian concept, which maintains that large firms are more innovative as a result of market imperfection and technological capitalization (Marimuthu et al., 2009).

A good number of researchers have addressed the issue of organizational capital investment relative to job performance (Davila et al., 2006; Nelson & Pack, 1999). However, these researchers failed to provide a critical assessment of the impact of organizational capital investment on employee innovation. After a comprehensive review of related literature, the theory that stands out on this topic is that organizational capital investment is a critical input in the production of valuable human capital (Hacklin et al., 2006). It is important to point out specifically that the gap in the literature as reviewed is that research has not been conducted regarding the impact of capital investment on employee innovation. The researcher of the current study aimed to explore this as a new theory to contribute to the field of business administration. Therefore, the problem statement points to the fact that it is not known how organizational capital investment impacts employee innovation in the manufacturing industry. Additionally, this research will shed more light on how organizations identify and create the appropriate capital investment, and promote an enabling environment that is conducive for employee innovation (Davila et al., 2006). Adamson (2009a) and Swanson (2001) stressed that firms invested greatly in programs designed to enhance and inspire employees with innovation-oriented corporate culture. Keeley (2006) gave a broader theoretical perspective on how innovation links to technology and employee performance in terms of general characteristics. This type of corporate culture can be achieved by providing rational support and a climate conducive to employee innovation (Carmeli, Reiter-Palmon, & Ziv, 2010; Davila et al., 2006; Keeley, 2006).

Manufacturing companies face stiff foreign and domestic regulatory threats; consequently, they become exposed to brand imitations that are aided by weak regulatory laws (Davila et al., 2006). Under this condition, organizational leadership structure and hype become critical to employee innovation. Hence, a strategic management tool, such as a SWOT analysis or total quality management (TQM), can be employed to stay ahead of such competitive pressures (Keeley, 2006).

Aside from having a strong financial posture, a company's employee innovativeness can equally be a source of strength when it is commercialized (Davila et al., 2006). It stands to reason that creative ideas can be gainful and beneficial to both the organization and society at large when they go through the innovation process and products are commercialized (Amabile, 1997). There have been many creative thinkers and innovators who could not reap the benefits of their creative ideas due to some organizational drawbacks (Henry, 2001). A case in point is the X-ray scanner that was invented by EMI Company but was commercialized by another company, General Electric (Henry, 2001). Another instance is the VCR that was invented by Ampex/Sony but was gainfully commercialized by another company, Matsushita (Henry, 2001). The pragmatic moves taken by both the General Electric and Matsushita are exactly what defines innovation, or putting creative ideas into profitable objective reality (Henry, 2001). This assertion was effectively demonstrated by Black and Decker and Xerox Corporation using the Corning's Five-Stage Stage Gate production management theory to revamp their production processes (Petroy, 2007). The strategy is, primarily, to remain competitive (McCrillis & Salamie, 2005; Petroy, 2007).

Innovation can emanate from creative ideas, and creative ideas can be enhanced by the application of technology in the form of organizational capital investment (Tether et al., 2005). There is little consensus among researchers concerning research designs and worldviews relative to a capital investment measurement approach (Corbin & Strauss, 2008). For example, Merriam (2009) posited that "there is almost no consistency across writers on how, the philosophical aspect of qualitative research is discussed" (pp. 120-125). She also noted that each researcher, using a qualitative approach, tends to make sense of the field relative to a personal and socially constructed perspective, thus limiting the tendency of reflexivity. Stewart (2010) employed a human resource (HR) approach in measuring and managing intellectual capital, thus using the total productivity measure, revenue divided by employees, and using operating income divided by employment costs as an output measure (pp. 121-124). Conversely, Phillips (2005) posited a different value system in the utility of employees, thus providing a human investment option to enable executives to make an informed decision regarding human capital investment.

As Fitz-enz (2009) rightly remarked in his book titled, *The ROI of Human Capital*, the importance of human capital cannot be overemphasized in light of the fact that employees are just like any other assets that need to be carefully monitored and managed. Fitz-enz addressed the issue of company investment in human capital, but with little or no emphasis on how much a company should expend on capital investment (e.g., machinery and monetary capital) to enhance employee innovation or performance. In other words, Fitz-enz did not address why it is important to pay special attention to capital investment and determine the actual level of returns on capital investment relative to employee innovation. He also did not address the necessary measures to be considered. This means the quest to identify the impacts of organizational capital investment on employee innovation should be seen as a valuable tool for enhancing employee innovation, a prime factor in increasing a company's competitive advantage and revenue base (Phillips, 2005).

On the other hand, it can be argued that people find it extremely difficult to change because they are naturally resistant to change. Hence, it is the environment that changes. Consequently, it leads to the paradigm that says, "Businesses have to change the way they operate in order to increase their revenue base, and competitive advantage" (Phillips, 2005, p. 13). This assertion may justify the proposition that complex organizational problems can be solved with greater ease and in less time through the application of organizational capital investment, such as the use of equipment by engineers to aid in designs and computers to ensure improvements in operational effectiveness as opposed to manual application (Phillips, 2005). This means that when discussing the impact of capital investment on employee innovation, it is necessary to determine the role of management in enhancing innovation (Phillips, 2005). The employees are the major element in any business organization imbued with the capacity to maintain organizational competitiveness and generate the required revenue (Phillips, 2005). Other factors, such as machinery, plant, and equipment, may serve in an auxiliary capacity (Phillips, 2005, p. xix).

Generally, it stands to reason that the ability of organizations to innovate is predicated on the ability of those in management to make an informed capital investment decision and create an appropriate culture that enhances employee innovation (Bendis & Byler, 2009).

The current research was therefore based on phenomenology that entailed an exploration of the lived experiences of the subjects. In this case, the methodology involved audio-taped interviews as the primary data collection method (Creswell, 2007; Denzin, 2010). The interviews were made up of open-ended questions to enhance the gathering of rich and pertinent data (Creswell, 2007). The interviews were formulated to explore the lived experiences of a purposeful sample of 16 professional managers who had a background in manufacturing plants and a minimum of 5 years of on the job experience. The sample included male or female engineers, marketing managers, accounting managers, financial managers, and production/operational managers who were involved in financial, design, production, and marketing activities related to the finished products in various manufacturing plants. In view of the above background analysis, this research involved a phenomenological study using qualitative approach that emphasized the lived experiences of the subjects (Corbin & Strauss, 2008).

Theoretical Foundation

The theoretical foundation was built on the literature review with particular reference to the concepts that can help to present a clear understanding of the issues related to the impact of capital investment on employee innovation. These concepts can be harnessed to achieve sustainable innovative goals (Corbin & Strauss, 2008). The review of the literature showed that organizational capital investment can be considered a critical input in the development and production of valuable human capital (Adamson, 2009a; Foucault, 2008). Therefore, the gap in the literature points to the fact that research has not been conducted on the impact of organizational capital investment on employee innovation in the manufacturing industry. Moreover, the problem statement clearly points to the fact that it is not known how organizational capital investment impacts employee innovation in the manufacturing industry. Hence, the researcher of this study proposed to explore this as a new theory to contribute to the field of business administration. Generally, it stands to reason that the ability of organizations to innovate is predicated on management's capacity to make an informed capital investment decision and create the appropriate culture that can enhance employee innovation (Bendis & Byler, 2009).

It should, however, be clearly understood that the driving force in this study was the overall research question of, Does organizational capital investment impact employee innovation? This is considered to be the overarching question that formed the basis of the analytical part of this study (Adamson, 2009a; Becker, 2004). The analysis, inevitably, synchronized with the framework of the research by incorporating pertinent literature and theories, such as the human capital theory to support the significance of the overall RSQs:

RSQ1: What are the most important factors that are favorable for employee innovation?

RSQ2: What are the most critical elements of organizational capital investment?

RSQ3: Are there any managing challenges regarding capital investment and employee innovation?

These RSQs helped to explore the extent to which capital investment impacts employee innovation in the manufacturing industry. The appropriate theory that underpins this study is the theory of the wise allocation of resources, which is discussed fully in a later section of this chapter. It presents a potential for obtaining a microscopic insight into the organizational capital investment process as it impacts employee innovation (Adamson, 2009a). However, some researchers employ both the aggregate indices and monetization models to validate needed transformation (Corrado et al., 2004). In the aggregate indices model, a number of factors are considered to establish an overall innovation indicator, while in the monetization approach, employee innovativeness can be measured as a dollar value based on the innovation activities (Corrado et al., 2004). Arundel (2007) treated expenditures on intangible assets as investments in innovation capacity.

An appreciable amount of literature documents how employee performance compares with organizational capital investment. For instance, Creswell (2007) and Ichniowski and Prennushi (1997) maintained that ideas can be put into innovative process to the best advantage of companies. Also, organizational capital investment, such as plant and machinery, can be correlated with economic growth. This correlation portends that mere factors of production are not sufficient enough to unleash economic prosperity without employee innovative input (Nelson & Pack, 1999).

The concept of innovation is quite complex, and the complexity depends on its application coupled with various forms of organizational frameworks. However, innovation is a successful and gainful exploitation of creative ideas (Hacklin et al., 2006). The idea behind employee innovation is to create low risk opportunities and enhance competitive advantage (Pham, 2010). Innovation can be seen as a form of new product creation and service delivery, as well as a process that aligns capital investment with employee resource to increase value proposition (Tidd et al., 2005).

It would suffice to mention specifically that the general weakness prevalent in the literature review is the fact that researchers failed to take into account the factors that contribute to employee innovation (Creswell, 2007; Nelson & Pack, 1999). Tidd et al. (2005) posited that taking a holistic view of such factors would probably make a significant difference in business outcomes. Furthermore, the literature synthesis revealed that there is a growing investment in human capital as a driver to employee innovation (Fitz-enz, 2009; Hacklin et al., 2006; Pham, 2010; Tidd et al., 2005). However, there is inadequate evidence that corroborates the impact of organizational capital investment on employee innovation. The propensity for organizations to innovate is predicated on management's ability to create the appropriate technology coupled with the right environment for employee innovation to flourish (Davila et al., 2006). Therefore, future studies must be re-conceptualized and strategies evaluated more carefully to bridge this gap and identify important factors that promote organizational competitiveness, productivity, and growth.

Theories and Models Relating to Capital Investment and Innovation

Theory of Capital Investment

The theory of capital investment, as presented by Harris and Raviv (2002) clearly explains the direction capital investment should be pursued and made relevant, which will lead to value/profit maximization. It presents a roadmap that many business managers have embraced relative to firm size, a resource to enhance employee performance and innovation (Harris & Raviv, 2002). However, the implications of this model have to do with failure to take into account the debt contract that helps to determine the capital structure. Hence, existing debt can make organizational capital investment less attractive (Harris & Raviv, 2002).

Tournemaine, Grimaud, and Chantrel (2012) and Stadler (2012) examined the complementary in investment in human capital at a micro level, using a reduced form of econometric concept and theoretical model. Courvisanos (2007) employed a continuous time model to analyze investment in human capital and employee skills. In this case, investment in human capital can be pursued to acquire skills required for organizational capital investment, and investment in R&D can increase productivity by leveraging employee innovation. This model adopts differences in investment cost behavior across firms in relation to differences in the firm profitability (Courvisanos, 2007). The continuous time model helps to explain the impact of capital investment spending on labor productivity through skill acquisition.

Theory of Human Innovation

Tournemaine et al. (2012), using the innovation and human capital theory, explained that high costs of recruitment in relation to the scarcity of skilled labor tend to weaken the incentive to innovate. Also, lower capital investment leads to lower innovation that reduces the economic return accruing from employee innovation, a model that sheds light on the determinants of gaps in the educational achievement and employee innovative goal (Mumford, Hester, & Robledo, 2011).

Using the autonomous innovation model, China, for example, adopts this model as a way of developing and using domestic technology to manufacture goods locally (Crawford & Di Benedetto, 2008). In 2008, China established the Commercial Aircraft Corporation of China (CACC) primarily to promote an indigenous civil aviation manufacturing industry so as to compete favorably in the global market with Boeing and Airbus in the United States (Crawford & Di Benedetto, 2008). It stands to reason that a firm's key competitive advantage is its employees; hence, capital investment helps to attract talent that leads to innovation and impacts the company's profitability (Hamel, 2012).

As articulated by Stiles and Kulvisaechana (2004), organizational competitive advantage is dependent not, as originally assumed, on natural resources, economies of scale, or technology, given the fact that these are increasingly easy to imitate. This notion is built on the theory of a resource-based view (RBV) as later seen by Cool and Dierickx (1993). Contrary to the RBV theory, technology can be considered analogous to organizational capital investment. In other words, one cannot talk about technology and human capital in isolation of organizational capital investment. It stands to reason that human capital in the form of employee innovation is of no intrinsic value when it is not tapped and commercialized, a function attributable to organizational capital investment (Park, Gardner, & Wright, 2004).

The theory of the wise allocation of resources, as espoused by Adams et al. (2006) and Courvisanos (2007), points to aligning anything that creates the best product value to the organization. This is in conformity with the theory relating to capital investment and employee innovation designed to identify the ideal balance for a particular firm in a particular context (Adams et al., 2006). This will also help to identify how to apportion limited resources between different innovational needs of a firm. The response to this search can lead to management and collaboration advantages (Courvisanos, 2007). This means tapping employees' creative capabilities by identifying appropriate ways to embark on capital investment in an effective, competitive, and profitable manner (Courvisanos, 2007). This, of course, poses a serious challenge to management in terms of finding the appropriate strategies for apportioning capital investment in machinery and equipment that aligns with employee innovation performance (Appelbaum, Habashy, & Shafiq, 2012).

Review of the Literature

In the current world of discontinuous change, there is no continuity in the absence of constant renewal (Hamel, 2012). In the past, most managers of large businesses were unable to delineate their corporate innovational needs, especially in the areas of organizational capital investment and employee innovation (Appelbaum et al., 2012). Today, a good number of large business organizations are committed to both technological capitalization and employee innovation, realizing that business flourishes based on the ability to devise a new strategy for capital investment (Hamel, 2012).

Additionally, Appelbaum et al. (2012) maintained that achieving and sustaining high levels of employee performance requires a positive workplace environment and practices that leverage employees' knowledge and ability to create value. They maintained that specific capital investment strategies should be tailored to fit different industries and occupations in terms of employee innovative processes, training, and knowledge-sharing (Appelbaum et al., 2012). These various innovative practices can be more effective when they are implemented together and in concert with appropriate capital investment strategies (Appelbaum et al., 2012). However, it is important to reiterate that the gap in the literature as reviewed is that research has not been conducted regarding the impact of capital investment on employee innovation. This study sheds more light on the following: (a) how organizations can identify and create the appropriate capital investment, and promote an enabling environment that is conducive for employee innovation; and (b) identify how employee innovation can be considered a component of return on investment (ROI; Davila et al., 2006).

Keeley (2006) and Godin (2005) stressed that firms invest greatly in programs designed to enhance their innovativeness, thus inspiring employees with an innovation-oriented corporate culture. Evidence has shown that business organizations tend to place more emphasis on how skills drive innovation but give little or no attention to how capital investment impact employee innovation (Godin, 2005; Keeley, 2006). Businesses need to innovate constantly in order to stay competitive and sustainable (Keeley, 2006). This explains why capital investment is considered to be an important driver of employee innovation. Hence, the resources expended in R&D can be attributable to employee innovation (Keeley, 2006). Similarly, the physical product value arising from R&D is considered as the output, a key factor in determining the impact of capital investment on employee innovation (Jorgensen & Irmer, 2011). However, exogenous factors, such as capital output ratio, advertising intensity, concentration, and size of the industry, can account for differences in employee innovation in small and large firms, especially those that have over 500 employees (Solow, 2007). Invariably, manufacturing companies face stiff foreign and domestic regulatory threats (Solow, 2007). They are open to brand imitation as a result of competitive pressure and weak regulatory laws (Solow, 2007). In this case, the issues of organizational leadership structure and hype are critical to employee innovation. This is because strategic management tools, such as a SWOT analysis and TQM, can be employed to stay ahead of such threats (Keeley, 2006). On the other hand, a company's employee innovativeness can equally be a source of strength as well as an opportunity when commercialized (Keeley, 2006). This is to say that creative ideas can be gainful and beneficial when they go through the innovation process and are commercialized (Hacklin et al., 2006). To buttress this assertion, there have been many creative thinkers and innovators who could not reap the benefits of their innovativeness due to some organizational draw backs or what may be called *disruptive technology* (Christensen, 2003; Godin, 2005; Henry, 2001).

Accidents are crucial to innovation, such as in processes, design, and products. For example, Alexander Fleming accidentally discovered Penicillin mold in 1928 and its anti-bacterial agent which he called penicillin (Thota & Munir, 2011). Subsequently, this discovery revolutionized the idea of treating infection in humans with antibiotics (Thota & Munir, 2011). There have also been discoveries in technological fields, such as the microwave, ovens, and photography (Thota & Munir, 2011). Austin and Lee (2006) argued that in turning accidents into innovation, companies need to embrace serendipitous opportunities. In other words, companies need to target innovative employees and design appropriate capital investment that matches their innovative strength. To buttress this concept, Cisco acquired a number of smaller firms with new technologies in different stages of operation (Thota & Munir, 2011). The idea was to develop and tap into employee innovation, as well as use it as a platform to penetrate and expand into a new market (Thota & Munir, 2011).

As Fitz-enz (2009) rightly remarked in his book titled, *The ROI of Human Capital*, the importance of human capital cannot be overemphasized in light of the fact that employees are just like any other assets that need to be carefully monitored and managed. It can also be argued that people find it extremely difficult to change because they are naturally resistant to change; hence, it is only the environment that changes (Phillips, 2005). This perception leads to the paradigm that says, "Businesses have to change the way they operate in order to increase their revenue" (p. 11), a situation attributable to employee innovation (Fitz-enz, 2009). The perception may also justify the proposition that complex organizational problems can be solved in less time and with greater ease through appropriate capital investment, such as the use of computers to ensure improvements in operational effectiveness as compared to manual application (Phillips, 2005).

Summary
As noted earlier in this chapter, in today's world of discontinuous change there is no continuity without constant renewal (Hacklin et al., 2006). This is true in the sense that many researchers consider employee innovation to be one of the most vital characteristics every business organization should embrace (Jorgensen & Irmer, 2011; Thota & Munir, 2011). It therefore stands to reason that a company's competitive advantage is built on the innovative vision of its employees, given the appropriate leadership (Runco, 2007).

This review of the existing literature revealed that large firms are committed to various forms of innovation, including employee as well as technological, radical, and transformational (Runco, 2007). Yet, when managers of these firms were asked to describe their corporate innovation system, almost none of them could do it (Runco, 2007). This means organizations need a well developed strategy capable of maximizing capital investment resources and employee innovativeness (Runco, 2007). This is a major management challenge (Hamel, 2012). Similarly, Adams et al. (2006), in his theory of the wise allocation of resources, argued that organizational capital investment can be allocated in ways that enhance employee innovation. Jorgensen and Irmer (2011) claimed that more emphasis should be placed on capital investment as a critical source of employee innovation as well as a means of increasing value and market demand. In terms of measurable factors,

Brest and Hamilton Krieger (2010) asserted that resources expended in R&D should be considered to be a key output factor in the value measurement of employee innovation (Jorgensen & Irmer, 2011). These divergent findings, as revealed in the literature review, support the need for the current study. The focus of the current study was on: (a) the factors favorable for employee innovation, (b) the determinants of capital investment, and (c) management challenges to capital investment and employee innovation in the manufacturing industry.

Businesses have flourished based on the fact that they were able to devise new business models and identify new sources of revenue orchestrated through change in technology and employee innovation (Hamel, 2012). Therefore, the theoretical framework model used in the current study can be likened to the theory of wise allocation of resources (Adams et al., 2006). This theory examines the impacts of organizational capital investment on employee innovation, with particular reference to the collaboration between organizational entrepreneurship (the engine of inspiring vision) and scarce resources (capital investment and employee innovativeness) as a construct to the overall research question as stated in the chapter. This serves as a platform or channel that mirrors the direction of this study. In terms of measurable factors, the resources expended in R&D were considered as the key output factor for the value measurement of employee innovation (Jorgensen & Irmer, 2011).

Also, tangible capital investment, such as plant and equipment, was taken into consideration. Researchers in this discipline, as revealed in the literature review, have a number of issues with data collection for measuring organizational capital investment, but such issues are not unique (Haskel & Wallis, 2013). Evidence has shown that these issues emanate from the fact that researchers focus on data of activities when measuring organizational capital investment. Hence, it does not present a best way of measure (Haskel & Wallis, 2013). It therefore stands to reason that the ideal theory to enhance this research study was the theory of the wise allocation of resources as espoused by Courvisanos (2007). This means tapping employees' creative capabilities by identifying appropriate ways to embark on capital investment in an effective, competitive, and profitable manner (Courvisanos, 2007).

Chapter Three

Methodology

There are three main types of research: qualitative, quantitative, and mixed methods (Creswell, 2007). Each method has different philosophical assumptions relative to worldviews, and the type of research dictates the applicable methodology (Creswell, 2007). This research involved the use of a qualitative approach and the design entailed in-depth interviews, as they are considered optimal for collecting data in a phenomenological study (Smith, Flowers, & Larkin, 2009).

The use of qualitative research methodology has exceptional advantages in comparison to the quantitative approach (Smith et al., 2009). This is mainly because qualitative research has the capacity to probe into participant responses to elicit additional explanations relative to the phenomenon under study, such as beliefs, behaviors, and experiences (Denzin, 2010; Smith et al., 2009). In other words, a qualitative research approach helps to provide answers to the "how" and "why" questions presented in the open-ended interviews (Denzin, 2010).

Research Questions

The overall research question used to guide this study was: Does organizational capital investment impact employee innovation in the manufacturing industry? It should be noted that the data collected from the RSQs were analyzed to address and provide an answer to the overall research question (Booth et al., 2005; Creswell, 2007; Richards & Morse, 2007). This concept is referred to as triangulation (Creswell, 2007).

The RSQs that were considered in this study were as follows:

RSQ1: What are the most important factors that are favorable for employee innovation?

RSQ2: What are the most critical elements of organizational capital investment?

RSQ3: Are there any managing challenges regarding capital investment and employee innovation?

Research Methodology

This research was based on phenomenology. In other words, it involved an exploration of the lived experiences of the subjects (Creswell, 2007). However, it is important to mention that this phenomenological study can be considered a special case study because it focused not only on one particular site, but one group of professional managers from different manufacturing plants in Baltimore, Maryland. Potential participants were selected through a convenience and purposive sampling method using the researcher's personal professional network and met the following criteria: male or female engineers, marketing managers, accounting managers, financial managers, or production/operational managers who were 25 years or older, had 5 years of on the job experience, and had a minimum of a high school diploma.

The research design employed was a qualitative study utilizing semi-structured interviews, audiotape, primary data collection, coding, and analysis (Creswell, 2007; Denzin, 2010). This research also included a theoretical framework that connected all other aspects of inquiry into the entire study (Smith et al., 2009). In other words, sufficient data from multiple sources, primary and secondary, dealing with previous studies on capital investment and innovation were collected and synthesized for verification purposes (Denzin, 2010). The focus was on a population of 65 individuals from the researcher's personal network of male and female engineers and managers who were involved in the entire production and marketing aspects of the products in their various manufacturing plants in Baltimore, Maryland. The gender makeup comprised both males and females who were 25 years or older and held a minimum of a high school education.

Research Design

An appropriate purposeful sampling method suitable for a phenomenological approach was used to ensure variations in the male and female employees who were interviewed (Denzin, 2010). The major factors of interest in the overall research question were organizational capital investment and employee innovation. The conceptual framework included semi-structured interviews and informal conversations with individuals from the researcher's personal network of engineers and managers. A sample of 16 professional engineers, and managers comprising both males and females with a minimum of 5 years of on the job experience was interviewed. The managers included marketing managers, accounting managers, financial managers, and production/operational managers. The composition was chosen to ensure that the researcher interviewed all those connected with the company's organizational capital investment, employee innovation, and profitability.

Population and Sample Selection

A sample of 16 professional managers was drawn from a population of 65 managers and engineers from various manufacturing plants in Baltimore, Maryland. The researcher contacted each participant at a convenient location, outside their places of employment, to collect their personal contact information such as names and phone numbers. he demographic makeup of this sample comprised both males and females who were 25 years or older and held a minimum of a high school education. The researcher scheduled an appointment with each participant at a convenient location to explain the contents of the consent form prior to the interview. Each participant signed the consent form. The researcher collected the signed consent form and proceeded with the list of interview questions for data collection. The sample participants were interviewed and the resulting data were extracted and analyzed to provide an answer to each of the research questions. The interview lasted for 45 minutes with each participant. This enabled the researcher to gain a clear understanding of whether or not organizational capital investment impacts employee innovation.

Data were drawn from both senior and middle level professionals, including engineers and managers who were actually involved in the design, production, marketing, and sales of goods. The minimum required work experience was 5 years with the industry.

Instrumentation

The duration of the interview with each participant was 30 to 45 minutes. The researcher used note taking, audio recording, and follow-up questions, if deemed necessary, during the process of the interviews to ensure the accuracy and reliability of information. Three types of interview questions were used to address the overall research question. The data and information collected were used to accomplish the statement of purpose and objective of the research as stated in Chapters 1 and 2.

Demographic questions (DQs). Demographic questions were asked of each participant before the actual interview questions. This helped the researcher to collect data to describe the participants. The demographic questions were as follows:

DQ1. What is your gender? (Male or female)

DQ2. What is your age? (25-34 years old, 35-44 years old, 45-54 years old, 55-64 years old, 65 years or older)

DQ3. What is the highest degree or level of education you have completed? (High school graduate, diploma, or GED; Some college credit, no degree; Associate's degree; Bachelor's degree; Master's degree; Professional degree; Doctorate)

DQ4. How long have you been working with this company? (1-5 years, 6-10 years, 11-15 years, 16-20 years, 21 years or above)

Interview questions (IQs). Interview questions were comprehensive questions directly asked of each participant in the course of the interview. The interview questions were designed based on the overall research questions. The interview questions were as follows and can also be found in Appendix A:

IQ1. What are the most important factors that enhance your employee innovation? (Please rate the effectiveness of each choice: high, medium, or low).

IQ2. How does organizational capital investment impact employee innovation?

IQ3. How does your company promote its employee innovation?

IQ4. What is the approximate turnover rate of your employees?

IQ5. What is the strength of your company's workforce?

IQ6. What was your company's gross expenditure on capital investment equipment and R&D in 2008 and 2010?

IQ7. What was your company's total turnover in 2012 and 2014?

IQ8. How would you rate the effectiveness of your company's employee innovative support?

IQ9. How long have you been working with this company, and in what capacity?

IQ10. What do you consider as the most critical determinants of capital investment?

IQ11. Why do you think that organizational capital investment is important?

IQ12. In what ways do you think your company can innovate?

IQ13. What do you suggest can be done to enhance employee innovation?

IQ14. What are the innovative goals of your company?

IQ15. What are the innovation strategies that would help your company to achieve its goals?

IQ16. What are the managing challenges to your organizational capital investment?

IQ17. What do you consider as challenges to capital investment in machinery and equipment?

IQ18. What are the managing challenges to employee innovation in your company?

IQ19. Do you consider organizational capital investment as significant player toward employee innovation? If so, why?

IQ20. What do you as an engineer/manager have to change to enhance innovative performance in your organization?

IQ21. What are the challenges you encounter in your department regarding employee innovation?

IQ22. How does organizational capital investment impact productivity of your company?

IQ23. What are the best employee innovative policies of your company?

IQ24. What management style would you consider suitable for employee innovation?

IQ25. Do you consider under-capital investment as a pitfall in employee innovation?

Follow-up questions (FQs). Follow-up questions were asked of each participant depending on how they answered the interview questions. The follow-up questions were kept handy should the need arise.

Quality Criteria

Quality in qualitative research is not judged by rigor and scientific value, but by evaluation criteria, such as credibility in terms of value, applicability in terms of transferability, consistency in terms of dependability, and neutrality in terms of conformability (Smith et al., 2009). However, this is not to say that a qualitative design lacks limitations; the fact remains that qualitative designs have limitations and no one particular approach or design is considered the best (Corbin & Strauss, 2008; Smith et al., 2009). All research requires due consideration of various factors when dealing and choosing the appropriate design (Corbin & Strauss, 2008).

Rigor was assured in the current study by making sure the methodology and processes were credible, dependable, and transferable. This is true in the sense that Ryan, Coughlan, and Cronin (2007) suggested that credibility, dependability, transferability, and goodness be used to support rigor in qualitative research. However, Corbin and Strauss (2008) posited that phenomenological analysis does not rely on participant review or findings to establish qualitative rigor.

In terms of credibility, there was prolonged engagement with the subjects. In other words, the researcher was involved in conducting all interviews. The study participants were given the opportunity to ask questions prior to the commencement of the interviews. The study was approved by the Institutional Review Board (IRB) prior to commencement. A consent form was provided to each participant (See Appendix B) and confidentiality pledged as participants were fully informed about the nature of the study (Creswell, 2007).

In terms of transferability and goodness, this study was concise and well written both in grammar and organization (Corbin & Strauss, 2008). Also, the findings are appropriately presented and descriptive information clearly stated to give readers insight indicating that the interpretations therein were in line with data analysis (Creswell, 2007). However, the researcher should not hesitate to caution about certain limitations relative to resources and time constraints. The researcher warned about potential complications in collecting data from participants; hence a replication of the study would be desirable. Therefore, the basic sources of data in qualitative research are mainly through interviews and documents (Corbin & Strauss, 2008).

Reliability and Validity

It was believed that relevant descriptions of the phenomenon of this study could be achieved with a qualitative research approach (Corbin & Strauss, 2008). The basic qualitative design deemed suitable for this study was an in-depth open-ended interview. However, the qualitative research questions of "why?" and "how?" were used to generate pertinent answers for the research interview questions, primarily to understand the socially constructed reality of respondents (Denzin, 2010). The researcher made sure that participants were not influenced in what they said by keeping personal contact with the study participants throughout the duration of the study.

Reliability in this research was assured by using the same interview questions for different study participants in a pilot test. The purpose was to elicit uniformity in response and to help fine tune the research questions accordingly (Denzin & Lincoln, 2011). Validity was ascertained with the writing and recording of responses from respondents during the interview.

Data Collection Procedures

Primary data were drawn from a sample of 16 selected professional managers and engineers selected through a convenience and purposive sampling method using the researcher's professional network. The snowball method was also used to seek more participants from these individuals' referrals. All contact was made through personal contact information only. The techniques of data collection in this research began with in-depth semi-structured interviews, note taking, audio recording, and follow-up questions, if deemed necessary, with the participants. Additional data were collected by phone where face-to-face contact could not be established due to some obvious reasons.

The content of the interviews and other pertinent information was recorded and summarized into a content sheet. Multiple responses were allowed for each question. Respondents were handed a list of interview questions to indicate their responses.

The idea of adopting multiple data sources accounts for the cross-checking and validating of data (Denzin, 2010). These processes formed the basis on which conclusions were drawn. The final data collection was generated based on the research questions and interviews as indicated in Table 1.

Table 1

RSQs vs. Interview Questions

RSQ	Interview Questions (IQ)
RSQ 1: What are the most important capital investment factors that enhance employee innovation?	IQ1. What are the most important factors that enhance your employee innovation? (Please rate the effectiveness of each choice: high, medium, or low). IQ2. How does organizational capital investment impact employee innovation? IQ3. How does your company promote its employee innovation? IQ4. What is the approximate turnover rate of your employees? IQ5. What is the strength of your company's workforce? IQ6. What was your company's gross expenditure on capital investment equipment and R&D in 2008 and 2010? IQ7. What was your company's total turnover in 2012 and 2014? IQ8. How would you rate the effectiveness of your company's employee innovative support? IQ9. How long have you been working with this company, and in what capacity?
RSQ 2: What are the most critical elements of organizational capital investment?	IQ10. What do you consider as the most critical determinants of capital investment? IQ11. Why do you think that organizational capital investment is important? IQ12. In what ways do you think your company can innovate? IQ13. What do you suggest can be done to enhance employee innovation? IQ14. What are the innovative goals of your company? IQ15. What are the innovation strategies that would help your company to achieve its goals?

(continued)

Table 1 (continued)
RSQs vs. Interview Questions

RSQ	Interview Questions (IQ)
RSQ 3: Are there any managing challenges regarding capital investment and employee innovation?	IQ16: What are the managing challenges to your organizational capital investment? IQ17. What do you consider as obstacles to capital investment in machinery and equipment relative to employee innovation? IQ18. What are the managing challenges to employee innovation in your company? IQ19. Do you consider organizational capital investment as significant player toward employee innovation? If so, why? IQ20. What do you as an engineer/manager have to change to enhance innovative performance in your organization? IQ21. What are the challenges you encounter in your department regarding employee innovation? IQ22. How does organizational capital investment impact productivity of your company? IQ23. What are the best employee innovative policies of your company? IQ24. What management style would you consider suitable for employee innovation? IQ25. Do you consider under-capital investment as a pitfall in employee innovation?

Procedure

The researcher scheduled an appointment with each potential participant at a convenient location to explain the contents of the consent form. Each participant agreed to sign the consent form and handed it over to the researcher before proceeding with the list of interview questions for data collection. Audiotape recording was used during the interviews. Audiotaped responses were translated and analyzed using software such as NVivo. Coding was used to safeguard the identity of each participant. Data were coded and analyzed using flow charts, bar charts, and tables to display results. Hardcopies will be shredded or pulped for recycling, and digital files will be deleted or purged.

Data Analysis Procedures

The first step in the analysis, after the collection of data, was the transcription and printing of responses to each question on a separate sheet of paper. Codes were used to ensure the proper identification of each respondent (Denzin, 2010). The responses were sorted into groups according to similarity of content and the groupings were reviewed for clarity and validity. The audio taped interviews were transcribed and analyzed using qualitative software, such as NVivo. This helped to manage the data and assist in coding and compiling flow charts to show connections between codes (Smith et al., 2009).

Descriptive statistics, such as graphs and tables, were used to analyze the research questions. Coding is an important part of the analysis process. Codes refer to names, tags, labels, or any nomenclature coined by the researcher to facilitate the analysis of data (Patton, 2002). The data represent notes, memos, and other written information from field interviews. Coding was used to assign meanings to large amounts of text, words, phrases, sentences, paragraphs, and passages. What is important in data collection and analysis is the ability to convert the data into meaningful information and use this information to make an informed decision (Solow, 2007). The data collected from the RSQs were analyzed to address and provide an answer to the overall research question (Booth et al., 2005; Creswell, 2007; Richards & Morse, 2007). This concept is referred to as triangulation (Creswell, 2007). Analysis was conducted using tables and figures to illustrate the age range of respondents, gender, education, and experience. The measures are summarized in Table 2.

Table 2
RSQs vs. Data Analysis

RSQ	Data Analysis (DA)
RSQ 1: What are the factors favorable for employee innovation?	Analysis used descriptive statistics, such as tables and figures. Coding was also used to assign meanings to large amounts of text, words, phrases, sentences, paragraphs, and passages to capture the factors favorable for employee innovation.
RSQ 2: What are the most critical elements of organizational capital investment?	Analysis used descriptive statistics, such as tables and figures. Coding was also used to assign meanings to large amounts of text, words, phrases, sentences, paragraphs, and passages to capture capital investment factors.
RSQ 3: Are there any managing challenges regarding capital investment and employee innovation?	Descriptive statistics were employed to determine and describe patterns in the data using tables and figures. Coding was also used to assign meanings to large amounts of text, words, phrases, sentences, paragraphs, and passages related to managing challenges.

Ethical Considerations

Informed Consent

Consent in research is a federal regulation adopted by institutions of higher learning. It requires all research studies involving interaction with human participants, regardless of whether or not identifying information is being used, to be submitted to an IRB for approval. Respondents gave their informed consent prior to participation in the interviews. In order for respondents to give informed consent:

- The researcher informed the respondents of the purpose of the study, content, duration, and potential risks and benefits involved.
- The researcher made it clear to the respondents that it was not mandatory that they answered all of the interview questions.

- The researcher also informed the respondents that they had the option to opt out at any point in the course of the study.

In order to obtain consent for this study, a formal application for approval of informed consent was made to the IRB. The informed consent means informing participants of the risks, benefits, and procedures involved in the study. Upon approval, the consent form was given to all participants to read, sign, and date if they were in agreement with the terms and conditions of participation in the research study. The signed copies of the form, as well as all other related interview documents, will be kept by the researcher for a period of 3 years (Jorgensen & Irmer, 2011).

Confidentiality and Anonymity

It is imperative that researchers keep respondents' identities confidential. To ensure confidentiality, researchers should not link respondents' identifiers to their interview or survey responses when using data. Common identifiers include respondents' names, social security numbers, telephone numbers, and addresses.

Limitations of the Study

The study had certain limitations that were out of the researcher's control. They were as follows:

- There was a time constraint in which the researcher needed to complete the dissertation research.
- There was a financial constraint in completing the dissertation research.
- The researcher had no control over the responses the participants provided to the interview questions.
- The study was limited to one firm, making it hard to generalize the results.

Delimitations of the Study

Delimitations refer to conditions over which the researcher has control and uses to set the boundaries of the study. They were as follows:

- A sample of 16 professional engineers and managers, mostly from one industry (manufacturing only) in Baltimore, Maryland, was used.
- The employees came from the manufacturing industry only, with a minimum of 5 years of on-the-job experience.
- This was a qualitative study.

Summary

It is believed that relevant descriptions of phenomena in social sciences, market research, and other academic disciplines can be achieved with a qualitative research method (Corbin & Strauss, 2008). Basic qualitative designs that were considered for this study include semi-structured interviews, field notes, and audiotape. Qualitative research questions of "why?" and "how?" can be used to generate reasons that govern certain behaviors, primarily to understand a socially constructed reality (Corbin & Strauss, 2008).

The qualitative methodology used in this study served as a source for data collection using the appropriate research design. The RSQs were clearly defined using semi-structured interviews. The data and information generated from the RSQs were managed, analyzed, and triangulated to provide reasonable answers to the overall research question (Creswell, 2007; Richards & Morse, 2007). This was highlighted with the use of tables and figures.

Reliability and validity measures were designed to ensure trustworthiness in the final outcome. This means both the researcher and the end users can be assured that the findings are a true reflection of what the study was designed to accomplish (Lincoln & Guba, 1985).

Potential Benefits of the Study

Participants

Participants in this study were not given any personal incentive or compensation for their participation, monetary or otherwise. In short, other than a sense of making a contribution to the study, there was little and no immediate benefit to the participants. However, the study findings may lead to:

- A reduction in product price due to an increase in product quality, enhanced process, and competition

- New product innovation
- Price differentiation

Professional Community

The results or outcomes of this study may benefit the professional community, including policymakers, prospective researchers, and practitioners. The potential benefits cannot be overemphasized as those in the professional community may deem it necessary to incorporate capital investment and employee policy into their business models with the aim of increasing organizational competitive advantage and profitability. Results shed more light on previous related studies and add to the body of knowledge.

Chapter Four

Results

Restatement of the Purpose

The purpose of this study was to explore the impact of organizational capital investment on employee innovation in the manufacturing industry. The study was designed to address the unanswered questions confronting the leaders of many firms in this competitive global economy. That is, the problem of whether or not organizational capital investment impacts employee innovation. The review of literature indicated that most manufacturing organizations tend to place much emphasis on how skills drive innovation, but pay little or no attention to how organizational capital investment impacts employee innovation (Adams et al., 2006).

Therefore, the overarching question used to guide this study was: Does organizational capital investment impact employee innovation in the manufacturing industry? This study was intended to help address the aforementioned unanswered and overarching question.

Restatement of the Problem

- It is not known how organizational capital investment impacts employee innovation.
- It is not known how organizations identify and create the appropriate capital investment, and promote an enabling environment that is conducive for employee innovation (Davila et al., 2006).
- The gap in the literature as reviewed is that research has not been conducted regarding the impact of capital investment on employee innovation.
- A good number of researchers have addressed the issue of organizational capital investment relative to job performance (Davila et al., 2006; Nelson & Pack, 1999). However, these

researchers failed to provide a critical assessment of the impact of organizational capital investment on employee innovation.

Summary of the Study Methodology

Study Design

This study involved the use of a qualitative phenomenological case study design to probe the impact of organizational capital investment on employee innovation in the manufacturing industry.

Instrumentation

Data collection involved the use of personal interview questions, audio recording, and note taking. The researcher employed open-ended interview questions to elicit answers from the participants. Additionally, follow-up questions were used for clarity of purpose.

Participants

Participants were selected through a convenience and purposive sampling method, using the researcher's personal professional network, and needed to meet the following criteria: male or female engineers, marketing managers, accounting managers, financial managers, and production/operational managers who were 25 years or older, had 5 years of on the job experience, and had a minimum of a high school diploma.

The snowball method was also used to seek more potential participants from these individuals' referrals. All contact was made through personal contact information only. The researcher did contact each potential participant using the snowball method to collect their personal contact information, such as names and telephone numbers (information relating to their various workplaces was not collected); hence, permission was not needed from any organization or company.

The inclusion of participants from various departments within the manufacturing settings was designed to ensure the researcher interviewed all those involved in decision-making relating to capital investment, employee innovation, and profitability of the organization.

Participant Demographics

Demographic questions are designed to help researchers determine what factors may influence a respondent's answers, interests, and opinions. The participants' demographic information enabled the researcher to cross-tabulate and compares answers from different participants or subgroups. The total number of participants interviewed was 16, including nine males and seven females. The average age of the male respondents was 45.9 years, while the average age of the female respondents was 35.6 years. A summary of the participant demographics can be found in Table 3.

Table 3
Demographics of Participants

Respondent Code #	Job Title/ Occupation	Gender	Age Range	Job Experience in Years	Academic Level
1	Design Engineer	Male	44-54	5	Master's
2	Operational Manager	Male	35-40	6	Bachelor's
3	Production Manager	Female	30-35	5	Bachelor's
4	Production Manager	Male	45-54	6	Master's
5	Marketing Manager	Female	35-44	7	Bachelor's
6	Design Engineer	Female	35-44	6	Bachelor's
7	Accounting Manager	Male	45-54	8	Bachelor's
8	Operational Manager	Male	45-54	8	Master's
9	Marketing/ Sales Manager	Female	35-44	6	Bachelor's
10	Accounting Manager	Male	35-44	6	Bachelor's
11	Sales Manager	Female	35-44	5	Bachelor's
12	Human Resource Manager	Female	25-34	5	High School Diploma

13	Financial Manager	Male	55-64	6	High School Diploma/CPA
14	Design Engineer	Female	25-34	5	Master's
15	Financial Manager	Male	35-44	5	Bachelor's
16	Design Engineer	Male	35-44	6	Bachelor's

Research Sub Question 1

What are the most important factors that are favorable for employee innovation?

In order to find answer to RSQ 1, it is important to note that the participants in this study (i.e., engineers and managers) were interviewed because of their proven experience and persistent successful history of innovation in the manufacturing industry. Ideally, they represented various reputable manufacturing plants in the Baltimore area.

Interview question 1. The respondents were asked the following question: What are the most important factors that can enhance your employee innovation? (Please rate the effectiveness of each factor on a scale of 1 to 10 (See Table 4). Participants rated their answers on a scale of 1 to 10 (1 to 3 being extremely less important, 4 to 7 being important, and 8 to 10 being extremely most important). In analyzing the participants' answers, the researcher identified patterns in the data and developed categories that were integrated, moderated, and organized around two major factors—the application of appropriate cutting-edge technologies and modern management practices (See Table 4). This process of categorizing and tabulating data helped to provide the needed evidence to address the RSQs (See Figure 1 and Table 4).

The researcher observed that 55% of the respondents indicated the application of appropriate cutting-edge technologies was an extremely important factor that enhanced employee innovation; similarly, 45% of the respondents indicated that modern management practices were an important factor in the innovation of their employees as illustrated in Figure 1.

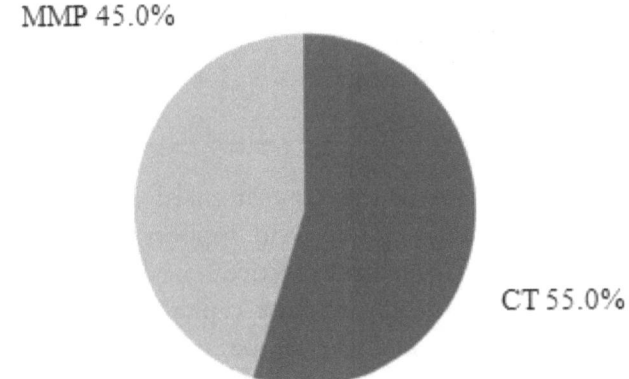

Figure 1. Modern management practices versus cutting-edge technologies.

Table 4
Respondents' Answers to Interview Question 1

Respondent ID #	Job Title/ Occupation	Scale of Importance (1-10)	
		Cutting-edge Technology	Modern Mgt Practices
1	Design Engineer	9	6
2	Operational Manager	8	5
3	Production Manager	9	6
4	Production Manager	9	5
5	Marketing Manager	6	8
6	Design Engineer	8	6
7	Accounting Manager	8	5
8	Operational Manager	9	6
9	Marketing/Sales Manager	6	8
10	Accounting Manager	8	6
11	Sales Manager	6	5
12	Human Resource Manager	6	8

13	Financial Manager	8	6
14	Design Engineer	9	5
15	Financial Manager	8	6
16	Design Engineer	9	5

Management practices in this context entail daily activities that managers employ to align, guide, and support employees in the production processes. Management practice is invaluable in a business organization because investors can raise capital and consumers can create demand for products and services, but managers play a vital role when it comes to developing the internal processes. In other words, management practices involve guiding and supporting employees and ensuring high performance and employee retention (Ray, Hyland, Dye, Kaplan, & Pressman, 2014).

It was also discovered during the interviews that these factors, as aforementioned, tend to increase and enhance safety in the workplace. This finding supports the fact that organizational capital investment does impact employee innovation given the application of appropriate technology and a modern management practice or business model. This assertion is in line with the notion supported by Warren and Susman (2004) and Afuah (2003) about innovation that clearly states, "Successful innovation is the use of new technological knowledge, market knowledge, and business models that can deliver a new product or service, or product/service combinations, to customers who will purchase at prices that will provide profits" (p. 5).

Interview question 4. The respondents were asked: What is the approximate turnover rate of your company's employees? The researcher asked respondents to rate their employee turnover rate as high, medium, or low (See Table 5). The researcher observed that 70% of respondents indicated their employee turnover rate was low at 5%, which indicates the employees were satisfied with their work. Therefore, job satisfaction may possibly be tied with a high employee retention rate, which is an important factor in employee innovation. It can be considered one of the ways that organizational capital investment may impact employee innovation; hence, a high employee retention rate is akin to the continuous creation of value and growth of wealth to benefit the broad population.

Interview question 5. Participants were also asked to indicate the strength of their company workforce (See Table 5). The researcher observed no remarkable trend in the company workforce and the rate of employee turnover given appropriate application of technology and modern management practices.

Table 5

Respondents' Answers to Interview Questions 4 and 5

Respondent Code #	Company Code #	Company Total Workforce	Rate of Employee Turnover		
			High	Medium	Low
1	A	2,500			X
2	B	2,000			X
3	C	1,500			X
4	D	1,800			X
5	E	1,500			X
6	F	1,200		X	
7	G	3,000			X
8	H	2,000		X	
9	I	1,500	X		
10	J	2,800			X
11	K	1,800			X
12	L	2,000			X
13	M	1,200	X		
14	N	1,600			X
15	O	2,500			X
16	P	1,800			X

As Table 6 indicates, all 16 participants responded to interview questions 6 and 7, "what was your company's gross expenditures on capital investment in equipment and R&D in 2008 and 2010?" Additionally, they were asked, "what was your company's total turnover in sales in 2012 and 2014?" The results indicated Company "B" had the highest expenditure in capital investment and R&D in 2008 and 2010, thus totaling $10.5 million and $12 million, respectively. In 2012 and 2014, this investment yielded total sales turnover of $22 million and $24 million, respectively.

Conversely, Company "K" had the lowest investment outlay on capital equipment and R&D in 2008 and 2010, at $4 million and $5 million, respectively. Consequently, in 2012 and 2014, the result of this investment yielded total sales turnover of $10 million and $15 million, respectively. In contrast, Company "B" apparently recorded an increase of $12 million (i.e., 100%) over what it expended on capital equipment and R&D in 2008 and 2010. It stands to reason that companies that invest more on capital equipment or R&D have the propensity to innovate their employees; hence, capital investment has a positive impact on employee innovation as well as the profitability of the entire organization. In summary, this result indicates investment in capital equipment has a direct relationship with turnover in sales due to product improvement.

Table 6

Respondents' Answers to Interview Questions 6 and 7

Respondent Code #	Company Code #	Gross Company Expenditure on Capital Investment ($Millions)		Company Total Turnover/ Sales($Millions)	
		2008	2010	2012	2014
1	A	$8	$10	$20	$25
2	B	$10.5	$12	$22	$24
3	C	$7	$10	$15	$20
4	D	$10	$12	$20	$24
5	E	$4.5	$8	$15	$18
6	F	$10	$10.5	$20	$22
7	G	$5.5	$8.5	$15	$18.5
8	H	$10	$10.5	$20	$24
9	I	$4	$6	$10	$12.5
10	J	$5	$7	$12	$14
11	K	$4	$5	$10	$15
12	L	$4	$5.5	$10	$15
13	M	$10	$8	$20	$24
14	N	$8	$10	$15	$20
15	O	$4	$6	$10	$15

16	P	$4	$5.5	$8	$10

Research Sub Question 2

What are the most critical elements of organizational capital investment?

To provide an answer to this RSQ, participants were asked the following interview question: In what ways do you think your company can innovate? Respondents' answers were as follows. RESP 1 stated "protection of intellectual capital by ensuring trade mark secrets, and patents protection." RESP 2 stated "high retention rate of employees" and "maintenance of competitive advantage over competitors." RESP 3 stated "knowledge acquisition" and "favorable work environment." RESP 4 stated "funding resource" and "ensuring conducive work environment."

Additionally, the researcher asked respondents the follow-up question of: Do you agree that organizational capital investment is the primary measure in which innovation diffuses through employees? As shown in Table 4, 45% of respondents believed appropriate management practices that include employee training and R&D are the most effective means in which innovation diffuses through employees.

As shown in Table 5, the researcher observed that the issue of recording a low employee turnover rate goes along with a favorable and conducive work environment. It was interesting to note that 80% of the respondents reported a "low" rate of employee turnover. The employee turnover rate indicates the speed at which employees enter and leave the company. A low employee turnover means employees are satisfied with their jobs, a condition favorable for employee innovation. This is in line with management practices mentioned in RSQ 1. Apparently, a company with a high employee turnover rate is one where employees do not retain their jobs for an acceptable period of time. The researcher deduced that organizational capital investment has a retention impact on employees. Therefore, management has the responsibility of putting employee engagement at the center of organizational activities and goals. It stands to reason that there is no organizational success without having a culture of team dedication and commitment.

Management practices such as communicating and developing a strong sense of direction and having a purview of what employees, customers, and all other stakeholders need is a recipe for profitability.

Businesses thrive when all stakeholders benefit (Mackey, Sismondi, & George, 2013). One of the greatest assets a company may have is the ability of managers to understand employees' strengths and be able to capitalize and leverage on those strengths (Buckingham, 2005).

Research Sub Question 3

Are there any managing challenges regarding capital investment and employee innovation?

Respondents were asked: What do you consider as obstacles to capital investment in machinery and equipment relative to employee innovation? The following responses were received. RESP 1 noted "the problem of under-funding." RESP 2 noted "harnessing and applying employee knowledge." RESP 3 stated "identifying and developing employee talents." RESP 4 stated "leadership challenges." RESP 5 stated "products and services challenges." RESP 6 stated "efficiency gap." RESP 7 stated "keeping pace with rapid technological changes." RESP 8 stated "no comments." RESP 9 stated "sources of fund." RESP 10 stated "rising labor cost." RESP 11 stated "product quality and efficiency." RESP 12 stated "competency level of workforce." RESP 13 stated "increasing cost of production." RESP 14 stated "coping with externalities." RESP 15 stated "scarcity of skilled labor." RESP 16 stated: "you be my guess."

A number of reasons were advanced by the respondents as critical challenges facing business organizations that attempt to eliminate product deficiencies through technological breakthroughs orchestrated by employee innovation. The responses point to the search for an ideal balance for a group of manufacturing firms in a particular context, and how to apportion their limited resources. Generally, all the responses boiled down to collaboration advantage and tapping the employee innovativeness that may impact organizational capabilities and profitability. Employee innovation can be influenced through training matched with appropriate technology. People talk about the greatness of companies such as Microsoft, GE, and General Motors, but forget that these companies did something quite extraordinary that made them so unique—–they capitalized on internal resources, such as focusing on capital investment and employee innovation (Ulrich & Smallwood, 2004).

Respondents cited "competency level of workforce," "skilled labor," and "keeping pace with rapid technological growth." The remedy to these challenges is for management to embark on a rigorous assessment of employees. A routine assessment of employee behavior relative to a task may help managers to determine the organizational capabilities and where to invest. In this way, employee capabilities can be matched with the company's innovation goals.

There is need for management to come up with decisions and actions that promote the company's capital investment needs that are in line with employee innovation levels. Such decisions may include targeting appropriate R&D programs and some structural changes to accommodate needed employee qualities. One of the greatest assets a company may possess is the ability of managers to understand employees' strengths and be able to capitalize and leverage on those strengths (Buckingham, 2005).

Summary

The impact of organizational capital investment on employee innovation as evidenced in this study can be summarized as follows.

Success and Growth of the Economy

The success and growth of the economy cannot happen in the absence of capital investment and employee innovation. This is true because when employee innovation is transformed into valuable tangible goods and services, consumer demand and interest are generated; consequently, jobs are created and the economy benefits (Pham, 2010).

Enhanced Employee Retention

Management practices such as communicating and developing a strong sense of direction and having a purview of what employees, customers, and all other stakeholders need is a recipe for sustainable productivity enhancement. Businesses thrive when all stakeholders benefit (Mackey et al., 2013). One of the greatest assets a company may have is the ability of managers to understand employees' strengths and be able to capitalize and leverage on those strengths (Buckingham, 2005).

Job Satisfaction

The success of any business organization hinges on getting the right people on the right job to ensure a high level of employee retention (Stewart, 2010).

Cost Reduction and Quality Improvement

The results revealed that 65% of the respondents believed cost reduction was one of the most important impacts of organizational capital investment on employee innovation. Additionally, quality improvement leads to improvements in market share through increased sales.

Enhanced Knowledge and Skills

As companies are constantly looking for new ways of doing business and improving product quality, brand, and design, they are open to accepting change in the workplace and embarking on R&D as a means of imparting new skills to employees.

Absence of Bureaucratic Bottleneck and Overhead

The absence of bureaucratic bottleneck and overhead tends to enhance employee satisfaction. Management practices should, therefore, have the tendency to impact employees, especially when the focus is directed toward innovation, empowerment, performance, and growth (Gittell, 2003).

Conclusion

Generally, it should be noted that this study reveals an interesting development regarding the impact of organizational capital investment on employee innovation. Organizational capital investment in relation to employee innovation can create values for the business by helping to transform, and enhance employee creative ideas that lead to their innovativeness. This elucidates the value-engineering that accrue from capital investment in plant and machinery resources. It stands to reason that capital investment can afford employees the ability to interact with appropriate technology in terms of innovative equipment in their respective career fields, and at the same time, developing their potentials through hands-on-experience. (Godin, 2005).

Chapter Five

Summary, Conclusions, and Recommendations

Background of the Problem

After a comprehensive review of literature related to the current study topic of the impact of organizational capital investment on employee innovation in the manufacturing industry, the theory that stood out on this topic is that organizational capital investment is a critical input in the production of valuable human capital (Hacklin et al., 2006). Therefore, the problem statement in the current study was that it is not known how organizational capital investment impacts employee innovation in the manufacturing industry. Result of this study shed light on how organizations identify the appropriate capital investment and promote an enabling environment that is conducive for employee innovation (Davila et al., 2006). Keeley (2006) gave a broader theoretical perspective on how innovation links with technology in terms of organizational capital investment. The general characteristics of this link demand that any innovative process tends to provide a meaningful solution to a problem (Keeley, 2006). The linkage in most cases results in valuable changes in the best interest of the organization relative to time and cost savings (Keeley, 2006).

Early theories on organizational capital investment were concerned with data collection for the measurement and adoption of appropriate business models. For example, Becker (2004) adopted firm level data while Black and Lynch (2004) adopted the establishment level data system. Becker, in his theory, could not establish that investment in employee education was analogous to employee innovation. In other words, it has not been clearly established that the value of employee innovation is a result of organizational capital investment in machinery and equipment (Corrado et al., 2004; Swanson, 2001; Tidd et al., 2005).

A synthesis of the literature also revealed that some researchers disagree with the notion that the availability of capital investment in equipment affords employees the opportunity to interact with innovators in their respective fields (De Angelis & Harvie, 2009; Swanson, 2001;

47

Tidd et al., 2005). Black and Lynch (2004) posited that the main problem with this theory hinges on the adoption of appropriate business strategies relative to organizational structure.

However, recent studies, such as those conducted by Hamel (2012), Thota and Munir (2011), De Angelis and Harvie (2009), Adamson (2009b), and Foucault (2008), point to the fact that organizational capital investment could have a vital impact on employee innovation when appropriately harnessed and managed. This theory lends support to the Schumpeterian concept, which maintains that large firms are more innovative as a result of market imperfection and technological capitalization (Davila et al., 2009; Marimuthu et al., 2009).

A good number of researchers have addressed the issue of organizational capital investment relative to job performance (Davila et al., 2006; Nelson & Pack, 1999). However, these researchers failed to provide a critical assessment of the impact of organizational capital investment on employee innovation. After a comprehensive review of related literature, the theory that stands out on this topic is that organizational capital investment is a critical input in the production of valuable human capital (Hacklin et al., 2006). It is important to point out specifically that the gap in the literature as reviewed is that research has not been conducted regarding the impact of capital investment on employee innovation. The researcher of the current study aimed to explore this as a new theory to contribute to the field of business administration. Therefore, the problem statement points to the fact that it is not known how organizational capital investment impacts employee innovation in the manufacturing industry. Additionally, this research sheds more light on how organizations identify and create the appropriate capital investment, and promote an enabling environment that is conducive for employee innovation (Davila et al., 2006). Keeley (2006) gave a broader theoretical perspective on how innovation links to technology and employee performance in terms of general characteristics.

Manufacturing companies face stiff foreign and domestic regulatory threats; consequently, they become exposed to brand imitations that are aided by weak regulatory laws (Davila et al., 2006). Under this condition, organizational leadership structure and hype become critical to employee innovation. Hence, a strategic management tool, such as a SWOT analysis or TQM, can be employed to stay ahead of such competitive pressures (Keeley, 2006).

Aside from having a strong financial posture, a company's employee innovation can equally be a source of strength when it is commercialized (Davila et al., 2006). It stands to reason that creative ideas can be gainful and beneficial to both the organization and society at large when they go through the innovation process and products are commercialized (Amabile, 1997). There have been many creative thinkers and innovators who could not reap the benefits of their creative ideas due to some organizational drawbacks (Henry, 2001). A case in point is the X-ray scanner that was invented by EMI Company but was commercialized by another company, General Electric (Henry, 2001). Another instance is the VCR that was invented by Ampex/Sony but was gainfully commercialized by another company, Matsushita (Henry, 2001). The pragmatic moves taken by both the General Electric and Matsushita are exactly what defines innovation, or putting creative ideas into profitable objective reality (Henry, 2001). It stands to reason that employee innovation is vital to a company's profitability when it is commercialized (Henry, 2001). This assertion was effectively demonstrated by Black and Decker and Xerox Corporation, using the Corning's Five-Stage Stage Gate production management theory to revamp their production processes (Petroy, 2007). The strategy is primarily to remain competitive (McCrillis & Salamie, 2005; Petroy, 2007).

Technology and industrialization have given rise to the globalization of trade, thus making it possible for the modern international community to initiate and embrace trade negotiations as championed by the WTO as well as other international and regional trading blocs (Manyika & Pelissie du Rausas, 2011). The idea is to remove trade barriers among trading partners and stimulate global economic growth (Manyika & Pelissie du Rausas, 2011). This stimulation of a global economy has produced a ripple effect, triggering the desire of leaders of MNCs to reconsider their organizational capital investment portfolios in relation to employee innovation (Manyika & Pelissie du Rausas, 2011). For example, the creation of the Internet accounted for significant growth in global productivity, thus adding about 3.4% to global GDP, a development attributable to employee innovation (Manyika & Pelissie du Rausas, 2011). Therefore, any discussion of the impacts of organizational capital investment on employee innovation will not be complete without reference to the technology and enterprise competitiveness that drive employee innovation (Marimuthu et al., 2009; Rastogi, 2002).

Innovation can emanate from creative ideas, and creative ideas can be enhanced by the application of technology in the form of organizational capital investment. The capacity of a firm to innovate, both in human resource and organizational capital investment (i.e., plant, machinery, and equipment), can be seen as a fundamental process toward the attainment of competitive advantage and economies of scale over other competitors within the same industry (Tether et al., 2005).

Employee innovation can be considered a natural phenomenon, though it can be complemented through the application of exogenous auxiliary resources such as technology, machinery, and equipment, thereby leading to organizational, human, and technological innovation (Pyka & Esben, 2013). This form of organizational philosophy tends to provide an enabling environment for firms to develop and exploit opportunities for employee innovation and eradicate inertia emanating from radical shifts in capital investment strategies and unfavorable technological changes. In the actual sense of the word, the term employee innovation portends creative resource and idea generation that leads to the transformation of values relative to the production of goods and services (Davila, Epstein, & Shelton, 2006).

There is little consensus among researchers concerning research designs and worldviews relative to capital investment measurement approach (Corbin & Strauss, 2008; Creswell, 2007). Stewart (2010) employed an HR approach in measuring and managing intellectual capital, thus using the total productivity measure, revenue divided by employees, and using operating income divided by employment costs as an output measure (pp. 121-124). Conversely, Phillips (2005) posited a different value system in the utility of employees, thus providing a human investment option to enable executives make an informed decision regarding human capital investment.

As Fitz-enz (2009) rightly remarked in his book titled, *The ROI of Human Capital*, the importance of human capital cannot be overemphasized in light of the fact that employees are just like any other assets that need to be carefully monitored and managed. Fitz-enz addressed the issue of company investment in human capital, but with little or no emphasis on how much a company should expend on capital investment (e.g., machinery and monetary capital) to enhance employee innovation or performance. In other words, Fitz-enz did not address why it is important to pay special attention to capital investment and determine the actual level of returns on capital investment relative to employee innovation. He also did not address the necessary measures to be considered. This means the quest to identify the impacts of organizational capital investment on employee innovation should be seen as a valuable tool for enhancing employee innovation, a prime factor in increasing a company's competitive advantage and revenue base (Phillips, 2005).

On the other hand, it can be argued that people find it extremely difficult to change because they are naturally resistant to change. Hence, it is the environment that changes and consequently leads to the paradigm that says, businesses have to change the way they operate in order to increase their revenue base, and competitive advantage (Fitz-enz, 2009). This assertion may justify the proposition that complex organizational problems can be solved with greater ease and in less time through the application of organizational capital investment, such as the use of equipment by engineers to aid in designs and computers to ensure improvements in operational effectiveness as opposed to manual application (Phillips, 2005). This means that when discussing the impact of capital investment on employee innovation, it is necessary to determine the role of management in enhancing innovation (Phillips, 2005). The employees are the major element in any business organization imbued with the capacity to maintain organizational competitiveness and generate the required revenue (Phillips, 2005). Other factors, such as machinery, plant, and equipment, may serve in an auxiliary capacity (Phillips, 2005, p. xix).

Generally, it stands to reason that the ability of organizations to innovate is predicated on the ability of those in management to make an informed capital investment decision and create an appropriate culture that enhances employee innovation (Bendis & Byler, 2009).

The interviews were made up of open-ended questions to enhance the gathering of rich and pertinent data. The interviews were formulated to explore the lived experiences of a purposeful sample of 16 professional managers who had a background in manufacturing plants and a minimum of 5 years of on the job experience. The sample included male and female engineers, marketing managers, accounting managers, financial managers, and production/operational managers who were involved in financial, design, production, and marketing activities related to the finished products in various manufacturing plants. In view of the above background analysis, this research involved a phenomenological study using qualitative approach that emphasized the lived experiences of the subjects (Corbin & Strauss, 2008).

Summary of Findings

In the literature review, the researcher observed that the business model can be employed as an interfacing function that helps to integrate internal and external organizational factors. The innovating employees and firms that were studied spent a considerable amount of resources and attention in capital investment initiatives, at the same time enhancing their intellectual capital (i.e., employee innovation). They did not hesitate in seeking partners across company boundaries.

It stands to reason that technology alone has no inherent value when it comes to the impact of organizational capital investment on employee innovation unless it is combined with other ancillary factors of production, such as marketing and sales, financial, and production or operational models. It is the combination of these factors of production that effectively impact employee innovation to deliver new products and services to consumers in the manufacturing industry. Hence, consumers will ultimately determine and purchase the new products and services at reasonable prices that guarantee profits to the manufacturers or producers.

The results of the interviews showed that organizational capital investment can impact employee innovation in several ways:

- Produce output impact: This has to do with the quality of the goods produced by employees as a result of collaboration and efficiency arising from capital investment. The role that such output plays in the economic life of consumers matters greatly; hence, such product efficiency plays a pivotal role in improving people's lives and satisfying market demand.
- Cost reduction impact: This has to do with the quality of goods produced at a lower cost.

- Operational impact: This pertains to both capital investment, social and health aspect of the employees, such as proficiency resulting from adaptability.
- Profitability: Resulting from economies of scale and competitive advantage, having a good share of the market within the industry.

The theoretical framework that underlies these assumptions depicts an important distinction between employees' innovational input arising from capital investment and the associated output inherent in employee innovation. For example, the discovery and use of the X-ray capital equipment in some hospitals across the country led to an innovative way of identifying certain diseases or ailments in the human body, which otherwise would not have been possible without the use or application of the X-ray equipment that is considered as capital investment (Henry, 2001). Similarly, the design of different models of automobiles would not have been possible without the use and manipulation of industrial power plants and equipment (Phillips, 2005). This also includes the revolutionizing of the current mode of transportation and electronic transfers, which has characterized the world of economics as a "global village."

In terms of quantifying the impact of capital investment on employee innovation, it may suffice to adopt the same standard applied to financial valuation; that is, Capital Investment Impact = Employee Innovation Benefits/Capital Cost. This formula may help to indicate the direction and cost effectiveness of a company's capital investment as it relates to employee innovation.

Therefore, to determine the capital investment impact on employee innovation, it may be best to approach it based on the cost of production per unit of expected employee innovation benefit or performance outcome (Stewart, 2010). In which case, the impact of capital investment on employee innovation can be equated with the value of production per unit of the expected employee benefit or performance outcome. For example, in a situation where an auto technician diagnoses a motor engine problem with the latest technological equipment, the assessment of benefit or performance outcome becomes the value per vehicle engine restored. The capital investment impact on the employee can then be measured based on the engine that was correctly restored. Simply expressed as: Capital Investment Impact = Engine correctly diagnosed. This takes into account the totality impact = employee innovation cost, as well as associated benefits. This theory can be expressed as: Capital Investment Impact = Capital Benefits or Employee Innovation. It stands to reason that the impact of capital investment can equally be assessed as a result of an increase in the quality and quantity of products arising from employee innovation, an outcome concept leading to the least cost of production per unit output. This includes the concept of the 5Ps—product, price, position, place, and packaging.

The theory of investment, as propounded by Keynes (1936), posits that underinvestment in capital leads to unemployment. This is true in the sense that underinvestment in capital has implications for consumption and savings. Hence, $Y = C + S$ (Y = Investment, C = Consumption, and S = Savings). The amount saved finally finds its way to the bank where it is used for investment in capital goods and other forms of investment. In this case, investment refers to the acquisition of new machines, power plant, and equipment.

Conclusions

Employee innovation in the manufacturing industry can be comparable to an airplane that needs wings to balance its landing gear; organizational capital investment provides this function. Many employees have valuable ideas that can be developed for the growth and profitability of the company, including all stakeholders. The result of this research shows that organizational capital investment can impact employee innovation through a combination of factors. In other words, there is no one definitive factor that can produce an overall positive impact on employee innovation. This is true in the sense that different manufacturing companies may have different objectives and goals. However, the ultimate aim of any business organization is to make profit.

The profit motive can be realized through various means or by a combination of factors depending on the employees and management's level of proficiency. Looking at it from the standpoint of economic vantage, one would deduce that organizational capital investment strategies in relation to employee innovation are generally not exclusive in nature and cannot be compromised for other alternatives. It stands to reason that organizational capital investment should not be benchmarked by mere monetary value, but by those factors that enable monetary value to be realized, such as management practices, marketing, quality improvement, customer satisfaction, job satisfaction, organizational culture, and R&D (Ray et al., 2014).

In summary, employee innovation is vital to the success and growth of industries and the economy. This is true because when employee innovation is transformed into valuable tangible goods and services, consumer demand and interest are generated. Consequently, jobs are created and the economy benefits (Ulrich & Smallwood, 2004; Pham, 2010).

Recommendation for Further Studies

Results of this research suggest that manufacturing companies should continuously embrace capital investment and improvement programs and invest in their employees. Profitability is about ensuring the highest rate of retention, innovation, and excellent customer service (Bersin by Deloitte, 2012).). It is important to note that the study design and sample size of participants used are not sufficient or large enough to determine with high degree of accuracy the extent to which organizational capital investment impact employee innovation in the manufacturing industry. It is recommended that future research be narrowed to a specific impact of organizational capital investment on employee innovation to determine the cost-effectiveness.

Also, the researcher recommends further probe into this topic, using quantitative methods, to ascertain whether the amount of organizational capital investment is proportional to the development of employee innovativeness. This will enable business organizations to channel their capital expenditure budgets appropriately.

References

Adams, R., Bessant, J., & Phelps, R. (2006). Innovation management measurement: A review. *International Journal of Management Review, 8*(1), 21-47.

Adamson, M. (2009a). The financialization of student life: Five propositions on student debt. *Polygraph, 21*, 107-120.

Adamson, M. (2009b). The human capital strategy. *Ephemera, 9*(4), 271-284.

Afuah, A. (2003). *Innovation management, strategies, implementation, and profits* (2nd ed.). Oxford, England: Oxford University Press.

Amabile, T. M. (1997). Motivating creativity in organizations: On doing what you love, and doing what you do. *California Management Review, 40*(1), 39-58.

Appelbaum, S. H., Habashy, S., & Shafiq, H. (2012). Back to the future: Revisiting Kotter's 1996 change model. *Journal of Management Development, 31*(8), 764-782.

Arundel, A. (2007). Inspiration survey indicators: What impact on innovation policy? In *Science, technology, and innovation indicators in a changing world: Responding to policy needs* (pp. 49-64). Paris, France: OECD.

Austin, R. D., & Lee, D. (2006). *Accident intention and expectation in the innovation process* [Working paper]. Cambridge, MA: Harvard Business School.

Becker, G. (2004). *Human capital: A theoretical and empirical analysis, with special reference to education.* Chicago, IL: The University of Chicago Press.

Bendis, R., & Byler, E. (2009, August). *Creating a national innovation framework: Building a public-private support system to encourage innovation.* Washington, DC: Center for American Progress.

Bersin by Deloitte. (2012, August 29). *New Bersin & Associates research shows high-impact learning organizations generate three times higher profit growth than their peers.* Retrieved from http://www.bersin.com/news/content.asp?id

Black, S. E., & Lynch, L. M. (2004). What's driving the new economy? The benefits of workplace innovation. *The Economic Journal, 114*(493), F97-F116. doi:10.1111/j.0013-0133.2004.00189.x

Booth, W. C., Colomb, G. G., & Williams, J. M. (2005). *The craft of research* (3rd ed.). Chicago, IL: University of Chicago Press.

Brest, P., & Hamilton Krieger, L. (2010). *Problem solving, decision making and professional judgment.* New York, NY: Oxford University Press.

Buckingham, M. (2005, March). What great managers do. *Harvard Business Review.* Retrieved from https://hbr.org/2005/03/what-great-managers-do

Carmeli, A., Reiter-Palmon, R., & Ziv, E. (2010). Inclusive leadership and employee involvement in creative tasks in the workplace: The mediating role of psychological safety. *Creativity Research Journal, 22*(1), 250-260.

Christensen, C. M. (2003). *The innovator's dilemma: The revolutionary book that will change the way you do business.* New York, NY: Harper Business Essentials.

Cool, K., & Dierickx, I. (1993). Rivalry, strategic groups and firm profitability. *Strategic Management Journal, 14*(1), 47-59. doi:10.1002/smj.4250140106

Corbin, J., & Strauss, A. (2008). *Basics of qualitative research: Techniques and procedures for developing ground theory* (3rd ed.). Thousand Oaks, CA: Sage.

Corrado, C. A., Hulten, C. R., & Sichel, D. E. (2004). *Measuring capital and technology: An expanded framework* (Finance and Economics Discussion Series, 2004-65). Washington, DC: Board of Governors of the Federal Reserve System.

Courvisanos, J. (2007). The ontology of innovation: Human agency in the pursuit of novelty. *History of Economics Review, 45,* 41-59.

Crawford, C. M., & Di Benedetto, C. A. (2008). *New products management* (9th ed.). Burr Ridge, IL: Irwin/McGraw Hill.

Creswell, J. W. (2007). *Qualitative inquiry and research design: Choosing among five traditions.* Thousand Oaks, CA: Sage Publications.

Davila, T., Epstein, M. J., & Shelton, R. (2006). *Making innovation work: How to manage it, measure it, and profit from it.* Upper Saddle River, NJ: Wharton School Publishing.

De Angelis, M., & Harvie, D. (2009). Cognitive capitalism and the rat race: How capital measures immaterial labor in British universities. *Historical Materialism, 17*(1), 30-33.

Denzin, N. (2010). On elephants and gold standards. *Qualitative Research, 10*(1), 269-272.

Denzin, N., & Lincoln, Y. (Eds.). (2011). *Handbook of qualitative research* (4th ed.). Thousand Oaks, CA: Sage.

Fitz-enz, J. (2009). *The ROI of human capital: Measuring the economic value of employee performance* (2nd ed.). New York, NY: Amaco.

Foucault, M. (2008). *The birth of bio politics: Lectures at the College De France (1978-1979).* (Trans Graham Burchell). New York, NY: Picador Press.

Gittell, J. H. (2003). *The Southwest Airline way.* New York, NY: McGraw-Hill.

Godin, B. (2005). *The linear model of Innovation: The historical construction of an analytical framework.* Retrieved from http:/www.csiic.ca/

Hacklin, F., Marxt, C., & Fahrni, F. (2006). Strategic ventures partner selection for collaborative innovation in production systems: A decision support system-based approach. *International Journal of Production Economics, 104*(1), 100-112.

Hamel, G. (2012). *What matters now: How to win in a world of relentless change, ferocious competition, and unstoppable innovation.* San Francisco, CA: Jossey-Bass.

Harris, M., & Raviv, A. (2002, July). Organization design. *INFORMS, 48*(7), 852-865.

Haskel, J., & Wallis, G. (2013). Public support for innovation, intangible investment and productivity growth in the UK market sector. *Economics Leyyers, 119*(2), 195-198.

Henry, J. (2001). *Creativity and perception in management.* London, England: Sage.

Jorgensen, B., & Irmer, B. E. (2011). A human capital framework: Designed for convergence. In M. Clarke (Ed.), *Readings in HRM and sustainability* (pp. 7-21). Prahran: Tilde University Press.

Keeley, L. (2006). *The power of innovation: 2006 VHA research series.* Chicago, IL: Doblin.

Keynes, J. M. (1936). *The general theory of employment, interest and money.* London, England: Palgrave Macmillan.

Lincoln, Y., & Guba, E. G. (1985). *Naturalistic inquiry.* Newbury Park, CA: Sage Publications.

Mackey, J., Sismondi, R., & George, B. (2013). *Conscious capitalism: Liberating the heroic spirit of business*. Boston, MA: Harvard Business School Publishing.

Manyika, J., & Pelissie du Rausas, M. (2011). *First quantitative assessment of the Internet's economic impact presented at e-G8 Forum*. Retrieved from http://www.mckinsey.com /videos/ video?vid=2372108314001&plyrid =2399849255001&height= 270&width=480

Marimuthu, M., Arokiasamy, L., & Ismail, M. (2009). Human capital development and its impact on firm performance: Evidence from developmental economics. *Journal of International Social Research, 2*(8), 266-270. Retrieved from http:/www. sosyalarastirmalar.com/

McCrillis, N., & Salamie, D. (2005). The Black & Decker Corporation. In *The international directory of company histories*. Retrieved from http://www.encyclopedia.com/topic/ The_Black__Decker_Corp.aspx

Merriam, S. B. (2009). *Qualitative research. A guide to design and implementation*. San Francisco, CA: Jossey-Bass.

Mexias, S. J., & Glynn, M. A. (1993). The three faces of corporate renewal: Institution, revolution, and evolution. *Strategic Management Journal, 14*, 77-101.

Mumford, D., Hester, K. S., & Robledo, I. C. (2011). Creativity in organizations' importance and approaches. In M. D. Mumford (Ed.), *Handbook of organizational creativity* (pp. 3-16). San Diego, CA: Academic Press.

Nelson, R., & Pack, H. (1999). The Asian miracle and modern growth theory. *The Economic Journal, 109*, 416-436.

Park, H. J., Gardner, T. M., & Wright, P. M. (2004). HR practices or HR capabilities: Which matters? Insight from the Asia Pacific region. *Asia Pacific Journal of Human Resources, 43*(3).

Patton, M. Q. (2002). *Qualitative research and evaluation methods* (3rd ed.). Thousand Oaks, CA: Sage Publications.

Petroy, A. R. (2007). *Inspiration through knowledge*. Trademarked lecture.

Pham, N. D. (2010). *The impact of innovation and the role of intellectual rights on US. productivity, competitiveness, jobs, wages, and exports*. Retrieved from https://www.infojustice.org

Phillips, J. J. (2005). *Investing in your company's human capital: Strategies to avoid spending too little, or too much.* New York, NY: AMACOM.

Pyka, A., & Esben, E. S. (Eds.). (2013). *Long term economic development: Demand, finance, organization, policy and innovation in a Schumpeterian perspective.* Berlin Heidelberg: Springer-Verlag.

Rastogi, P. N. (2002). Sustaining enterprise competitiveness – Is human capital the answer? *Human System Management, 19*(3), 193-203.

Ray, R., Hyland, P., Dye, D. A., Kaplan, J., & Pressman, A. (2014, October). *DNA of engagement: How organizations create and sustain highly engaging cultures.* New York, NY: The Conference Board.

Richards, L., & Morse, J. M. (2007). *Read me first for a user's guide to qualitative methods* (2nd ed.). Thousand Oaks, CA: Sage.

Ross, D. F. (1998). *Competing through supply chain management: Creating market-winning strategies through supply chain partnership.* Norwell, MA: Kluwer Academic Publisher.

Runco, M. A. (2007). *Creativity: Theories and themes: Research development practice.* Burlington, MA: Elsevier.

Ryan, F., Coughlan, P., & Cronin, P. (2007). Step by step guide to critiquing research: Part 1: Quantitative research. *British Journal of Nursing, 16*(11), 658-663.

Smith, J., Flowers, P., & Larkin, M. (2009). *Interpretive phenomenological analysis: Theory, method and research.* Thousand Oaks, CA: Sage.

Solow, R. (2007, May 21). *Heavy thinker: A review of Prophet of Innovation, Joseph Schumpeter and creative destruction.* Retrieved from http://www.newrepublic.com/article/heavy-thinker

Stadler, M. (2012). Engines of growth: Education and innovation. *Review of Economics, 63*(2), 113-124.

Stewart, T. A. (2010). *Intellectual capital: The new wealth of organizations.* New York, NY: Crown Publishing Group.

Stiles, P., & Kulvisaechana, S. (2004). *Human capital and performance: A literature review.* Cambridge: The Judge Institute of Management, University of Cambridge.

Swanson, R. A. (2001). Human resource development and its underlying theory. *Human Resource Development International, 4*(3), 299-312.

Tether, B., Mina, A., Consoli, D., & Gagliardi, D. (2005). *A literature review on skills and innovation: How does successful innovation impact on the demand for skills and how do skills drive innovation?* Manchester, UK: ESRC Center for Research on Innovation & Competition, University of Manchester.

Thota, H., & Munir, Z. (2011). *Key concepts in innovation.* Los Altos, CA: Palgrave Macmillan.

Tidd, J., Bessant, J., & Pavitt, K. (2005). *Managing innovation: Integrating technology, market, and organizational change* (2nd ed.). Chichester, UK: John Wiley.

Tournemaine, F., Grimaud, A., & Chantrel, E. (2012). Pricing knowledge and funding research of new technology sectors in a growth model. *Journal of Public Economic Theory, 14*(3), 493-520.

Ulku, H. (2004). *Research and development, innovation, and economic growth: An empirical analysis* (IMF Working Paper, 04/185). Retrieved from https://www.imf.org/external/pubs/ft/wp/2004/wp04185.pdf

Ulrich, D., & Smallwood, N. (2004, June). Capitalizing on capabilities. *Harvard Business Review.* Retrieved from https://hbr.org/2004/06/capitalizing-on-capabilities

Warren, A., & Susman, G. (2004). *Review of innovation practices in small manufacturing companies.* Retrieved from http://www.smeal.psu.edu/fcfe/

Appendices

APPENDIX A

Interview Questions

Interview questions are comprehensive questions, directly, asked of each participant in the course of the interview. The interview questions are designed based on the overall research questions. The interview questions are as follow:

IQ1. What are the most important factors that enhance your employee innovation? (Please rate the effectiveness of each choice: high, medium, or low).

IQ2. How does organizational capital investment impact employee innovation?

IQ3. How does your company promote its employee innovation?

IQ4. What is the approximate turnover rate of your employees?

IQ5. What is the strength of your company's workforce?

IQ6. What was your company's gross expenditure on capital investment equipment and R&D in 2008 and 2010?

IQ7. What was your company's total turnover in 2012 and 2014?

IQ8. How would you rate the effectiveness of your company's employee innovative support?

IQ9. How long have you been working with this company, and in what capacity?

IQ10. What do you consider as the most critical determinants of capital investment?

IQ11. Why do you think that organizational capital investment is important?

IQ12. In what ways do you think your company can innovate?

IQ13. What do you suggest can be done to enhance employee innovation?

IQ14. What are the innovative goals of your company?

IQ15. What are the innovation strategies that would help your company to achieve its goals?

IQ16. What are the managing challenges to your organizational capital investment?

IQ17. What do you consider as challenges to capital investment in machinery and equipment?

IQ18. What are the managing challenges to employee innovation in your company?

IQ19. Do you consider organizational capital investment as significant player toward employee innovation; if so, why?

IQ20. What do you as an engineer/manager have to change to enhance innovative performance in your organization?

IQ21. What are the challenges you encounter in your department regarding employee innovation?

IQ22. How does organizational capital investment impact productivity of your company?

IQ23. What are the best employee innovative policies of your company?

IQ24. What management style would you consider suitable for employee innovation?

IQ25. Do you consider under-capital investment as a pitfall in employee innovation?

APPENDIX B

Consent Form

BASIC CONSENT FORM

This study is being done by Hyacinth Nwachukwu who is a student in the Graduate School of Business and Management at Argosy University-Online working on a dissertation. This study is a requirement to fulfill the researcher's degree and will not be used for decision-making by any organization.

The title of this study is "The Impact of Organizational Capital Investment on Employee Innovation in the Manufacturing industry."

- The purpose of this study is to explore the impact of organizational capital investment on employee innovation.
- I was asked to be in this study because I met the criteria for participation: male or female engineers, marketing managers, accounting managers, financial managers, and production/operational managers who are 25 years or older, 5-year on-the-job experience, and a minimum of high school diploma.
- A total of 15-20 people have been asked to participate in this study.
- If I agree to be in this study, I will be asked to sign a consent form.
- This study will take approximately 30-45 minutes to complete
- The risks associated with this study are minimized through appropriate precautions that may prevent any possible physical, psychological, social, legal, economic or other risks to participants (such as follow-up calls to answer questions, and concerns, and/or referral to appropriate agencies when necessary).
- The benefits of participation are, primarily, to help provide answers that may enable the researcher to explore the impact of organizational capital investment on employee innovation in the manufacturing industry. It may, also, help to contribute to the body of knowledge in business administration.
- I will receive no compensation, monetary or otherwise, for participating in this study.

- All information provided must be treated confidentially, in other words, no other person except the principal researcher would be able to tell who I am.
- The records of this study will be kept private. No words linking me to the study will be included in any sort of report that might be published.
- The records will be stored securely and only the principal researcher, or dissertation chair, will have access to the records.
- I have the right to get a summary of the results of this study if I would like to have them. I can get the summary by contacting the researcher, Hyacinth Nwachukwu.
- I understand that my participation is strictly voluntary. If I do not participate, it will not harm my relationship with Argosy University – Online or the researcher. If I decide to participate, I can refuse to answer any of the questions that may make me uncomfortable. I can quit at any time without my relations with the university, job, benefits, etc., being affected.
- I can contact the researcher, Hyacinth Nwachukwu, or the dissertation chair, Dr. Matthew Kuofie at mhkuofie_gsmi@msn.com, with any questions about this study.

I understand that this study has been reviewed and Certified by the Institutional Review Board, Argosy University – Online. For problems or questions regarding participants' rights, I can contact the Institutional Review Board Chair, Dr. Nancy Hoover, at nhoover@argosy.edu

I have read and understand the explanation provided to me. I have had all my questions answered to my satisfaction, and I voluntarily agree to participate in this study. I have been given a copy of this consent form. By signing this document, I consent to participate in the study.

Name of Participant (printed)_____

Signature:_____Date:_____

Name of Principal Investigator:_____

Signature:_____Date:_____

Information to identify and contact investigator:
    Hyacinth Nwachukwu